John Wells

The Conspiracy

Vol. 1

John Wells

The Conspiracy
Vol. 1

ISBN/EAN: 9783337337469

Printed in Europe, USA, Canada, Australia, Japan

Cover: Foto ©Thomas Meinert / pixelio.de

More available books at **www.hansebooks.com**

THE

CONSPIRACY

A DRAMA.

G. D. HENRY, PRINTER,
JOHNSTOWN, N. Y.
1873.

THE CONSPIRACY.

Persons of the Drama.

The KING.
Dr. JOHN, *Greek Professor.*
The PRINCE,
PAUL,
FRANK,
MARK, } *Students.*
ERNEST,
ANGELO, *a Clairvoyant.*
JULIAN,
The PRINCESS, *Daughter of the King.*
ANNA, *Daughter of Dr. John.*
PAULINE, *Sister to Paul.*
Other Students, Citizens, Lords, Ladies, &c., &c.

ACT I.

SCENE I.—*A Grove in the grounds of a University.*

Enter FRANK, MARK, ERNEST, ANGELO, JULIAN, *and other Students.*

Ernest. This is the spot. We'll wait here, till he come.
Frank. There is old Plato. Bless his good old soul.
He has a heart to match his grand old head.
I doubt if ever towered a nobler brow
On Grecian statue. All heads bare. Hats off.

Enter Dr. JOHN.

Dr. John. Good morning, gentlemen ! What enterprise
Have you afoot, to signalize this day
And beauteous place ? It must be some high aim,
That in such brave array doth call you forth.

Frank. On deeds of high emprise are we intent.
Know'st thou of some fierce monster, to be slain,
Or beauteous damsel, wandering all forlorn,
In forest lost, or lonely captive kept,
In lofty tower, or dark, deep horrid cave,
By giant grim, or bloody baron bold ?
Oh ! speak ! that to the rescue we may rush.
    Dr. John. Monsters enow—of vice and wrong—
        there are,
And doubtless damsels in distress who sigh,
For valorous knights to rush to their relief.
But bearded champions they do prefer.
Wait, my dear sirs! till ye are out of school,
And have your beards ere ye adventure forth
On such achievements and essay to play,
The gentle knight a pricking on the plain.
But, speak, sirs! tell me, wherefore are ye here ?
    Frank. I will expound. You know, that by the course
Of antique custom, here by men renowned
Ordained of old——

Music heard

    Students. Hark ! Hush ! There's music here.
    Ernest. 'Tis floating in the air. Whence can it come ?
    Angelo. How sweet and spirit like it is !
    Dr. John.   It breathes
A strange, unearthly sweetness. It must be,
That in the air some gentle Ariel
Is hovering over us.
    Frank.   More like, 'tis Puck,
The merry fay. He's stole Æolus' lyre,
From off the pine upon the mountain top,
To practice on it airs of fairy land.
He seeks to lure us off to some lone place,
Some deep dark dell, or secret strange recess,
Amidst the forest, where the fairies haunt,
And where bewildered in the tangled wilds
We'll be within his power, for him, the imp,
To play his pranks and knavish tricks upon.
    Mark. Hist ! Hist ! The music dies away ! 'Tis gone !
    Dr. John. Now, speak, sir! Tell me wherefore are
        ye here ?

Frank. I will explain. You know that by the course
Of custom immemorial, in this
Most ancient seat of learning and of wit,
We students, here, to-morrow, publicly,
Must be, in scholarship and eloquence,
Examined by the learned men of the realm.
For genius and for learning, prizes rare,
Medals and marks of honor are in store ;
And he, who first in merit shall be found
Will be the heir unto a crown, a wreath,
That on his brow should by the King be placed—
E'en by the sacred hand of majesty.
But to the wars away the King has gone ;
And none is there to do this duty now,
But she, the lovely Princess, his fair child,
Whom in his place, he's left to rule the realm
As his imperial prototype, the sun,
When he doth visit the antipodes,
Doth by the moon, sweet regent of the night,
In gentle reflex of his mightier beam,
Still unto us dispense his blessed light.
Hence has our royal comrade, the good Prince,
The cousin of the Princess, gone to learn
From her, if she will take her father's place
And grace to-morrow's victor with his crown.
Oh ! doubly precious will the glory be
From her fair hand ! The Prince will soon be here
And we have come to meet him and to learn,
As soon as it may be, the word he brings.
Lo ! yonder comes he. Mercury ne'er sped,
Swift messenger of Heaven, with word from Jove,
To those who watched for him more eagerly.

The Music heard again.

Angelo. The music comes again. Hark ! how it swells
As from afar 'twere wafted down to us.
Hist ! Now it dies away, as up again
'Twere borne on viewless wings to airy heights.
It comes again ! 'Tis here !
 Mark.   'Tis here !
 Frank.   'Tis in the breeze !
 Angelo. There is some tricky spirit round, that seeks

With this sweet mockery to sport with us.

Dr. John.   There runs a thread of sadness through
the strain.
Methinks the harps of Judah hung upon
The willows by the streams of Babylon,
Though mute to Zion's songs, may to the winds,
That swept their chords, have breathed just such sweet
tones.

Frank. 'Tis some melodious zephyr in the trees.
Perchance some fancy-striken youth has strung
Among these leaves a lyre Æolian,
For the airy fingers to perform upon,
And these sweet airs, that thus salute our ears,
Are but the touches of the airs of Heaven.

Enter the Prince.

Students.   Hail to the Prince! Peace! Silence!
Let us hear.

Prince. Rejoice, comrades! Glorious the news I bring.
The Princess graciously doth grant our prayer.
To-morrow she will come with all her court
Of Lords and ladies fair and learned men,
To test our scholarship and eloquence.
In the evening, at the palace, she will give
In honor of our class, a festival ;
A royal one, whereto we all will go
And taste of earth's selectest revelry.

Frank.   Heaven bless our lovely Princess.

Mark.   As she's good
And beautiful, may she be ever blest.

Angelo. We'll see what Homer in his raptures saw,
When Venus, in her beauty walked before
Him on Olympus.

Frank.   There'll be a Hebe there,
Whom I shall see, with nectar—on her lips,
Sweeter than Jove e'er sipped.

Dr. John.   And doubtless all
The Graces will be there and troops of nymphs.
Invite a poet and the counterparts
He'll find to all the gods and goddesses.
Give it a Homer, and each age would be
Heroic, every mountain an Olympus.

Angelo. Heaven from its brightest constellations shed
On our sweet Princess happiest influence.

The Music heard.

Prince. What music 's this, that breathes so sweetly
     here?
Frank. 'Tis some enchantment, that doth haunt the
     place.
Prince. It softly swells, then dies upon the breeze,
Rising and falling with each airy wave.
It seems as from above afar it came.
Frank. The voice of harpers harping with their harps.
I'll bet the pearly gates are now ajar
And these sweet notes have thence escaped; or else
It is some genial spirit stolen forth
To have a laugh at us, some syren of
The golden harps come down to puzzle us
And to allure us with these hints of Heaven.
Prince. It is a strange peculiar melody.
But comrades! where is Paul, our gentle friend?
'Tis strange that he's not here.
Ernest.   We've seen him not.
Julian. As you do say 'tis strange that he's not here.
'Tis said, that he aspires unto the crown.
Perhaps his courage fails him and he yields
The prize to bolder aspirants—else sure
He would be here.
Prince.   I'll go and seek for him.
I've news, that will be music in his ears.
Frank. Hold! there's that strain again. 'Tis
     coming here.
Prince. It louder is, as if it nearer came.
Mark. Huzza! see there! see there! What tree
     is this,
That bears such fruit as that?

Paul discovered in the Tree.

Frank.   Ha! ha! Strange fruit indeed!
Some species new. Special spontaneous
Developement! Most like, on some such tree
Sprang forth that old primeval ape, that was
Our great ancestor. Darwin! Science that!

Or else : I have it now—a theory
Historical and theological,
And exegetical and pomological,
I do suspect, that 'tis the kind of fruit,
With which the serpent tempted mother Eve
In Paradise.
    Mark.   And all the mothers since.

Paul comes down from the Tree.

    Ernest. By all the powers and spirits it is Paul.
    Julian. By all the fiends and devils it is he.
    Prince. Art thou this spirit that's been mocking us
With this mysterious music so weirdlike ?
    Frank. Stick pins in him and see if 'tis real flesh
Or only some thin immaterial stuff.
Were any of Eve's daughters here, we'd let
Her take a bite and see what fruit it is.
    Julian (aside.) It is my dagger that I'd stick in him.
He is the only rival that I fear.
Were he out of the way, the crown were mine
With all the honors, that will come with it.
    Paul. Good friends 'twas but a jest—I will explain.
I had come out alone into this grove,
And here was sitting on this grassy bank,
Listening unto the music floating round.
And ever now and then upon my lute
I'd catch such notes from breeze, and brook and bird,
As struck my fancy. Thus it was I made
The little melody which you did hear.
Just then I saw you coming and I thought
I'd try my music on you. So I hid
In these thick branches, and as you came near,
I threw out on the breeze the notes you heard ;
It was their wild and fitful character,
Caught from the zephyr, that perplexed you so
And puzzled you to know, whence came
The mystic and uncertain harmony.
The jest succeeded better than I thought.
    Prince. 'Twas a most delicately merry jest ;
'Tis clear the zephyr did conspire with you
And instigate the mischief. But come friends,
We now must hasten back unto our work.

Think, what the morrow has for us to do !
> *Frank.* Of the bright eyes that on us then will beam.
> *Mark.* And the sweet smiles that with those beams
> will blend.
> *Ernest.* And of the honors that we there shall win.
> *Julian.* And of the crown that one of us will wear.
> *Prince.* And the fair hand that will bestow that crown,
> *Paul.* And of the honor of these ancient halls
Of learning, whose proud fame we must sustain.
> *Prince.* We'll make these groves and shades of ours
> renowned,
As were of old the walks of Academe.
> *Frank.* We'll leave our foot prints on the sands of
> time,
That when we have departed, seeing them
The world will say of us, " They walked with Plato."
> (*bowing to Dr. John.*)
Or, " Here (*to Julian*) was a Demosthenes," or " lo !
Here, (*to Angelo*) is a step Parnassian, on the heights
Where Homer stood," " Their (*to Paul and the Prince*)
> noble deeds
In lustre and true glory well might be,
Sisters unto those daughters, pure as fair,
Epaminondas left unto his country."
> *Dr. John.* Go on, Sir ! Socrates, Isocrates,
Xenocrates, Solon, Crates,
Aristides and Aristotles,
Thucydides and Sophocles,
Praxiteles and Pericles, and scores
Of starry ones ye well might name for bright
Comparison, for in her annals grand
Old Greece has specimens of every kind
Of glory.
> *Prince.* Come away ! To toil let's give the day,
That we our parts to-morrow well may play.
> *Exeunt,*

SCENE 2d.—*A Walk in the University Grounds.*

Enter FRANK, ERNEST and MARK.

Frank.   Wise as the serpent, harmless as the dove !
That means, we should use policy ;—should have
The spirit of the dove, its soul of love
And gentleness ; but with it should unite
The serpent's sharper qualities,—its tact,
Its keen-eyed, still, adroit and lowly art,
Its pliancy to bend to obstacles
And wind around them to its purposes.
Our aims should e'er be noble, to do good,
To make men happy and earth beautiful ;
But then to do all this,—to realize
These aims and work out these results of good
And beauty,—we must wisdom have, prudence
And policy ; or as the text doth bid,
The serpent with the dove we must combine.
To do things wisely, well, effectually,
Is just as much a duty, as it is
To do at all.   To go to Rome, we need
Not strike a bee-line, dig the Alps, or scale
The rocks and glaciers.   Rather we should shun
The perilous and craggy peaks and seek
The vales and trodden passes.   The right way
Is that, which surest leads to the right end.
The mountain paths wind up through the ravines.
At sea, the sailor trims his course to wind
And current.   So in all great enterprise
The occasion and the circumstance will best
Suggest the way.   For what is circumstance
But Providence ?   The winds He breathes, the waves
He lifts and rolls to waft or dash us on
Upon our destined way ?   Well, now,
We have in view an enterprise—a work
Before us for our country,—to achieve
Its liberty.   A noble aim, is't not ?
  Ernest. In every age the special work of heroes.
    Frank. To attempt it openly, were but to dash
Madly against the glaciers and the rocks

And wake the avalanche, to fight with it.
Hence from the serpent we must take our cue ;
Through thy dark winding ways, Oh ! thou wise snake,
Cunning Conspiracy ! creep stealthily,
But not less nobly onward to our end.
   Mark. Aye, policy and stern necessity
Both point it out, as our true only course.
   Ernest. I like it not. But it must needs be so.
Yes, anything and everything for country !
Yet, I do like it not. I'd rather give
Our banner to the winds and boldly march,
With shout and trumpet blast and cannon peal,
To victory or death. I like it not.
But anything I'll do, and everything
I'll dare, to win sweet liberty,
And make our dear, beloved country free.
   Frank. It is the motive, that gives character
Unto the act. A noble end
Ennobles every step, that leads to it.
In climbing mountains, we do bend and stoop,
And on the craggy steeps and slippery ways,
Oft on our knees creep up to glorious heights.
I have now in my mind a character,
One of the noblest spirits of the times,
Whose life has been one long conspiracy.
Hated and hunted of the tyrants, he
With plots and wiles has met and baffled them ;
His genius, zeal and purpose pure and high,
Mightier than were an army in the field.
In prison, exile, pain and poverty,
Yet has he been a power in the world,
A menace and a terror unto tyranny.
With pure, unselfish and untiring zeal,
He's toiled on, ever to his country true,
And to his great idea of liberty,
Alike the truest hero of the age,
And most inveterate conspirator.
   Mark. Aye, Italy, in all its long bright list,
Has not a name of purer lustre.
   Ernest. Tell me, how now do stand the citizens ?
   Frank. Eager for insurrection. Just ablaze.
The city's like a kindling fire ; a breath

Once blown, the flame of revolution forth
Will burst to startle and to light the world.
    Ernest. Has Paul yet given his assent ?
    Frank.   Not yet ;
But he'll be with us. We must have his name.
'Twere worth to us more than an armed troop.
By sweet attractive love and kindliness,
E'en as a sun 'mong men, he wins their hearts;
And good men circle round him planet-like,
And cluster in bright constellation. Thus
Doth earth present its counterpart to Heaven ;
Its asterisms of the good and wise,
High starry minds, pure natures like clear skies,
And shining galaxies of noble souls.
Aye, we must have his name and influence.
He'll be the Brutus of our enterprise.
    Mark. The Cassius thou. Your names as their's
       will be,
Like double stars blended in history.
Or greater still, ye'll be the Washington
And Adams of our revolution. Or
Epaminonidas and Pelopidas,
Of Grecian glory, your bright prototypes
We'll name, in what ye'll yet effect, we trust,
Of high achievement, for your country wrought
And proud renown.
    Frank.   There were two Adamses
With scores of patriots and noble men
Who stood with Washington. E'en so, of us
There'll be a cluster in the heaven
Of history.
    Ernest. But think you not, our friend
Is of a nature all too gently tuned ?
He's not of the stern mold that Brutus was.
    Frank. True, he's of gentle nature : Yet in him
There is the stuff, that heroes are made of.
I do remember, one dark gusty night,
When through the startled city piercing rang
The cry of "fire". The citizens, awaked
And guided by the glare, that lit the night,
Rushed to the conflagration. But too late.
A stately mansion stood, enwrapped in flames,

That seemed exultingly to sweep the skies
And bid defiance to the crowd, that stood
And gazed at them in sad stern impotence.
When, lo ! a woman's shriek did pierce our ears,
And swiftly, through the pallid multitude,
The whisper ran, that 'twas a mother's cry,
And that her babe was in the burning ruin.
The mocking fires smote back the rushing crowd,
That sprang unto the rescue.   Baffled shrank
Brave men, who had stood eye to eye with death.
And hope died in our hearts.   When suddenly
A youth appeared amidst the flames, that seemed
To seize him as their victim, as he leaped,
Fearless amidst them.   For an interval,
A breathless agonizing instant, he
Was gone, lost to our eager straining sight,
And the fierce conflagration wildly waved
Its crests upon the wind, as it had won
Another prey ; when, lo ! again he came,
And shook the flames from off him and did place
The sleeping babe upon its mother's breast.
That youth was Paul ; and even now the shouts
Ring in my ears, with which the people caught
Him in their arms and bore him home in triumph.
He's been their model hero since that hour.
There's slumbering a very iron mine
In him of force and dauntless energy,
From whence an Iliad of noble deeds
And high heroic action might be wrought.
This very night our club doth meet again.
Paul will be there and join with us and then
Within our influence and linked with us
In patriotic thoughts and aims, we soon
Will draw him into the conspiracy.
And then we'll make him captain and his name
And popularity will serve to win
Troops of good men and true, unto our cause.
                              Exeunt omnes.

SCENE III.—*A large room underground or cellar, fitted up with seats and with the emblems and symbols of the Club. A Skeleton in the highest seat. Present* FRANK *and* MARK. *Others coming in.*

Mark. It is a shapely, well developed skull.
Frank. A shapely, well developed spirit dwelt
In it. A true proportioned character :
With that just balance of the faculties,
That clear cut mold of fine pure elements,
That as a model, men could look at him,
And studying his qualities, learn what
True manhood was, and copying them
Make real the ideal in themselves.
His face was Truth's own mirror, where to look
To see herself, how pure and fair she was.
And wit and gladness were as natural
To him, as sparkles to a mountain spring,
Or ripples to a rill among the hills,
Or music to a well tuned instrument.
He was the founder of our Club, and when
He died, his body he bequeathed to us,
That we should cherish e'er his memory,
And think of him whenever we did meet,
E'en as in life we loved and honored him.
And so we did preserve his skeleton,
And voted it perpetual president.
Mark. A capital presiding officer !
Most august President ! We bow to thee.
Frank. There, so. Now let us see how he'll perform.

He pulls a spring, when it bows and reaches out its arms &c., &c.

Mark. 'Tis a most courteous and stately bow.
Frank. That is the grip initiate ;—and that
The squeeze of fellowship.
Mark.   A whole souled squeeze.
Frank. Here, sir ! Lift up your merry face. So. So.
Your skeleton's the true philosopher.
It grins, grins ever and at everything,
As having tried life, death, joy, pain, the grave,

It finds them all but matter for a grin.
  Mark. To that philosophy we'll all attain.

A Bell tolls. Enter ERNEST.

The bell tolls. It struck one. It is the time.
  Frank. Are they all here?
  Mark.   The number is complete.
  Frank, (*taking a seat beside the skeleton.*)
It is the hour. All please to order come.
We'll now commence the sacred mysteries.
'Tis first in order to initiate
New members.
  Ernest.   There is one who waits without,
Seeking to be admitted to our band.
  Frank. Into our presence let him now be brought.

They lead Paul in blindfolded and place him before the skeleton.

  Frank, (*addressing Paul.*)
Would'st thou become one of our brotherhood,
And give thy life up to the sacred work,
To which we pledge and do devote ourselves?
  Paul. 'Tis my desire so to devote myself.
  Frank. The aim of our Society is single;
And yet it has aims manifold. The first
The great peculiar end, to which all tends
Is to achieve our country's liberty.
For this as means unto this end, we pledge
Ourselves ever to closest secrecy;
That ne'er, beyond these ancient vaulted walls,
Shall breathe a whisper of these mystic rites.
Then, as a brotherhood, with holiest vows
Of friendship and affection, we do bind
Ourselves to cherish ever, each to each,
Pure faith and trust and gentle sympathy.
And we are vowed to live lives pure and high,
By no dishonor stained, or foul wrong deed,—
But to each generous, lofty aim devote;
That each one may, in life and character,
Exalt himself unto the loftiest reach
Of his capacity. Each one should be,
E'en as a Graecian statue, Phœbus-like
In form and look and action; and our lives

We'd make as dramas for Elysium writ,
Full of great thoughts, sweet scenes and noble acts,
Which they, the blest, might love oft to rehearse
For their high pastime, in the happy vales.
Is there a form of error in the world,
In custom, institution, or creed old,
'Tis ours to battle it.   Truth only may we heed.
Beauty for earth and happiness for man,
The motive and the aim of all our toil.
For this glad Liberty and gentle Peace
We'll strive to win, bright visitants from Heaven,
To make their dwelling here, with Science fair
And Art, bright clad, child of the earth and skies ;
Glorious Art, that yet shall gild our world,
In all its ways, with golden pavements, and
With beauty deck its bowers of blessedness.
But unto tyranny, and every form
Of slavery, we do swear unceasing war,—
A war to end only in victory.
Wilt thou unto these aims devote thyself
And join with us in a perpetual league?
    Paul.   Unto these lofty aims I pledge myself.
    Frank.   Canst thou, as on an altar lay thy life
And all its aspirations and fond hopes,
A willing offering to thy fatherland ?
    Paul.   Myself and all I am and all I have
Unto my country freely do I give.
    Frank.   Then, with uplifted hand and face to Heaven,
Swear thou, that to our order thou wilt be
A faithful brother, even unto death.
By Him whom thou dost reverence highest, swear.
    Paul.   I so do swear.   Faithful till death to be.
    Frank.   It is enough.   Invest him with the robe.

They put a robe and badge upon Paul.

Thou art our brother now.   Hold forth thy hand,
To give and take the grasp of brotherhood.

*Paul holds out his hand, when the skeleton's hand is placed in it,
and the veil is taken from his eyes.*

    Paul.   Is it with death I have clasped hands and vows
Of brotherhood exchanged ?   Aye, be it so.

Even to thee, oh Death ! I'll give myself
And willingly, if need be, by thy side
Lie down, to win my country's liberty.
Aye, comrades ! brothers ! I am with you now
And henceforth ever even unto death.
   Frank. Our noble brother ! Welcome to our arms
And hearts ! Thou with us, now our ranks are full,
Our number is complete. We need no more.

They crowd round Paul, shaking hands with him and singing.

> Give to us that hand of thine ;
>   With it, brother, give thy heart ;
> Holy is the tie that links us,
>   Death alone the links shall part.

> Lofty is our sacred mission ;
>   Hero workers we will be;
> Toiling for our Fatherland;
>   Fighting for its liberty.

> In each generous, high emprise,
>   Shall our banner be unfurled,
> And our motto ever be,
>   God, our country, and the world.

> Give us then thy hand, our brother !
>   One in heart and aim we'll be ;
> Nobly living, bravely dying,
>   Death be ours, or liberty.

                            Curtain falls.

SCENE IV.—*In the Palace. Guests assembled.* DR. JOHN, FRANK,
ANNA, MARK, ANGELO, JULIAN, *and other Students, Lords,
Ladies, &c., &c.* FRANK and ANNA *come forward.*

   Frank. The Princess comes. How beautiful she is !
   Anna. That's Paul with her. She leans upon his arm.
Ne'er by two arms was more of beauty linked.
   Frank. To me there's more now linked unto my arm.
Not for her crown would I exchange with him.
   Anna. No crown, nor wealth, nor rank to you I bring.
Nothing but poor, poor humble me you'll get.

But I will try and make it up in love.

Frank. In getting that, your love, I will get all.
'Tis more to me than all the world beside.

Anna. True, love is the best wealth. How rich we'll be!

*Enter the Princess and Paul, the Prince and Pauline and Lords
and Ladies at the upper end of the room.*

Frank. She now will crown him with his victor wreath.

Anna. 'Twas thought Count Julian would have won
the crown.

Frank. He strove for it and proved himself a ripe
Keen scholar, and with eager eloquence,
He did address us. But more grandly Paul
Did bear himself and spake as if inspired ;
As if some spirit through him uttered forth
Celestial thoughts and images. 'Twas so
The prophets must have stood, when they did speak
Of old, as through them poured in words of fire
The messages of Heaven. As I gazed
At him, while to the multitude, with eye
Afire and cheek ablaze, he spake, I thought
Of morning, when upon the hills it comes,
With golden locks and step of majesty,
And calls the waking nations. With a shout
The people hailed him and the Princess, as
Blushing she did award the prize to him.

Anna. Will she with her own hand bestow the crown?

Frank. With her own hand she'll place it on his brow.
And he will then select a queen, and they
Will be the monarchs of the festival.
He'll be a favorite. Mark the prophecy.

*The Princess comes forward with the Prince and takes her seat
upon the throne.*

Prince. May't please your Highness, the day's victor
waits
For his reward from your imperial hand.

Princess. Let him approach. Where is the garland?

*They hand her a wreath. The Prince, Frank, Mark and Julian lead
Paul forward. He kneels.*

Crowns should rewards of merit rightly be

And ever rest on really regal brows,
Regal by virtue of the royalty
Of brain and culture, mind and character.
May this be of thy triumphs but the first,
The least of many prizes won of glory.

She crowns Paul and leads him upon the throne.

This is your place to-night.   'Tis yours to reign
The monarch of our joyous festival.
The palace your dominion is, your will
Our duty and our pleasure to fulfill.
    Paul. Then shall my short lived reign be one of joy.
We'll steal an evening from the blessed isles ;
A plagiarism from Elysium.
I do decree, that every one partake
And help to swell the night's festivity.
Be joy the mark and measure of my sway.
The means of happiness to all be given.
Had I the power, I'd make all earth as Heaven.
But 'tis not good, for man to be alone,
And drear if solitary e'en a throne.
The sun divides his realm, bright king of day,
And with the queenly moon doth share his sway.
So will I have a queen to reign with me,
And with her smiles light our festivity.
    Princess. Look round ! Was lovelier vision ever seen ?
Choose whom thou wilt and she will be your queen.
    Paul. Of all the good, I'll have the very best,
And of the beautiful the loveliest.
The one, who shares my heart and throne, must be
Supreme in beauty, as in majesty;
Peerless in face and form, stately of mien,
Her will I choose.   Please you to be my queen.

The Princess gives him her hand.

The crown, wove tor the loveliest brow, give me.

They give him a wreath with which he crowns her.

The queen of beauty and of goodness crown I thee.
Right kingly now we'll wield our kingly powers,
And royally show forth our royalty.
Around the palace heap the tables high,

And bid all come unto our festival.
Proclaim it as the law, throughout our realm,
That every one to every other do,
As he would have that other do to him.
Invite the poets here, bid them devise
Some bright elysian game, some play of Heaven :
We will rehearse it here, that better there
We may act it hereafter.   Life should be
But a rehearsal of such acts and scenes,
As we may fitly yet react in heaven.
 Anna.   Have we no bards, like those of days of yore,
With songs to sing of love and chivalry ?
 Frank.   Songs are as gems, gendered in richest souls,
In which pure thoughts and sweet words crystalize.
They are as flowers, with which such souls bloom forth,
Blossoms of beauty and of melody,
Blooming and breathing sweetness ceaselessly.
 Dr. John.   Oh, for a song like those, that David sung !
Could he but come again and drink now of
The water of the well of Bethlehem,
How would he strike his harp to loftiest strains,
Sweeter than e'en of old, and Zion yield
To Calvary the palm of holy song !
 Frank.   A prayer ! a prayer, unto your majesties !
 Paul.   What is it ? speak ! if in our realm 'tis thine.
 Frank.   'Tis but a dance.   Bid the sweet music wake,
And lead a dance in which we all may join.
 Princess.   Would'st thou to vain and idle revelry
Have us give up these precious, golden hours ?
What can'st thou urge for such bold rash request ?
 Frank..   It is not vain and idle revelry.
Dancing is natural to man as song ;
And has in life its true significance,
Its purpose just and should have its due place.
It is akin to song and melody ;
Of the same pure and gentle parentage.
'Tis music acted—song in pantomime.
Music is of the soul and ever thence
It seeks expression.   It doth breathe itself
Forth in the voice, in concord of sweet sounds,
And then we call it song and melody.
In tuneful movements of the body, borne

Upon the flow of inner harmony,
It vents itself, and then 'tis dance,
Glad, joy inspiring dance. And in the march,
It is the soul swell, that uplifts the form,
And to heroic measures times the step.
Each an expression, song and dance and march
Of this soul music. Through all things doth breathe
This spirit of sweet harmony ;
And every atom of the universe
Is ever tremulous with uttering it.
The whistling winds come dancing o'er the hills,
And to the self same measures, as they come,
The groves do spring and all the billows leap,
In merry glee to join the revelry.
The stars do swing each other, as they fly,
And linked in shining orders, hand in hand,
Wheeling and whirling, dance upon their way.
And all their mighty, mystic maze—link wove
With golden link, worlds balancing to worlds,
Systems to systems, groups of glories bright,
And galaxies on galaxies in ranks
Illimitable, countless circles vast
Circling the eternal spaces, all are but
An infinite measure, ever wheeling there
And timing to immortal melody.
'Tis said, the fairies every moonlight night
Do have their frolic dances on the green.
And in the vales and groves of Arcady,
While fed the flocks upon the grassy banks,
The gentle shepherds, all the summer's day,
To pipe and harp and merry roundelay,
With nymphs and naiads danced the hours away.
And doubtless too, in the celestial fields,
Amid the hymning and the harping there,
By the still waters in the pastures green,
Angels and spirits blest, with raptures caught,
And borne on waves of wondrous melodies,
In dance inspired of grace ineffable,
May oft show forth the excess of bliss,
Else inexpressible, that fills their being.
In holy exaltation David danced,

With Israel, before the ark of God,
Upon its way to Zion,—with glad shouts
And hymns and peals of myriad instruments.
And dancing 'twas, he sang, " Worship the Lord
In the beauty of holiness". For praise
And prayer and song and dance and every act
Of gladness and of joy, in Him and in
His goodness, worship is, and doth show forth
Rightly the beauty of true holiness.
The man, that hateth dancing, mark him well,
He's of distorted temper. Bigotry
Hath bound its chain about him, fettering
The natural play and action of his spirit.
Some chord within his soul is out of tune,
Discordant, harsh, and gives not its true music.
Admit him not into your councils. He
Would in the purest fountains stir up slime,
And pluck from out life's garden the sweet flowers,
That God has planted there, to beautify
And gladden it. May not the lambs skip ? May
Not little children shout and sing and dance ?
And shall not we join with them in their joy ?
    Princess. I deem you've won your plea. I add my voice
To your petition.
    Paul.   'Tis granted. So be it.
Let music pour o'er us its fullest flood
And the glad dance float on its tide along.
We'll close no channel, in which joy can flow,
But rather open new ones, where we may,
And like the old Chaldean, leading forth
Amid his blighted plains, where Eden was,
In channels new and founts and sunny lakes,
The waters of the river, that at first
Had beautified and gladdened Paradise,
To win its primal beauty back again,
So would we multiply the reservoirs
And streams of joy amid life's wastes, to make
Them bloom anew and Eden smile again.

Music. *Paul and Princess, Prince and Pauline, Frank and Anna
and others dance.*

Julian. Jove could not bear himself more loftily.

He walks as if he were imperial born,
And all earth's royalty strode in his step.
See, how she smiles to him.   Aye, it is love.
Her soul is in each glance she turns to him.
Ha! Not a look she's given me this night.
Curse! Curse him! But for him that crown were mine
And with her I had led the festive dance :
But he has stole the honors I have sought,
For which I've toiled and would have given my soul,
And I must slink away, thus meanly here.
Would I could sheathe my dagger in his heart.
How the Prince eyes them with that yellow glare.
Perhaps he's jealous.   I will work on him.
I'll torture him and goad him to a rage
Of jealousy, and in his ear mean while
I'll whisper thoughts of mischief and revenge.
Thus with his pangs I will assuage my own.

Enter an Officer.

Frank. What news, sir! from the army and the King?
Officer. Such, as the Roman bore fled from who
    Cannae.
The cunning foe did lay his snares for us,
And madly did the King rush into them.
    Frank. Alas, for our brave army!
    Officer.   And alas
For our poor country!
    Frank. Well it were, brave sir!
Were we but rid of him.   'Tis our sole hope,
And happy for the country would it be.
    Officer. In this you but give voice unto a thought,
That's mute but universal.   Treason now
Is the best service patriots can give.
    Frank.   Let's step aside,
Where we may unobserved compare our thoughts.

Paul and Princess come forward.

Princess. The wreath you wear in my regard is peer,
To any diadem in Christendom.   [kind.
    Paul. Your words are gracious as your deeds are
Most truly do I render back my debt
Of gratitude and love.
    Princess.   Of love?

Paul.   Aye, love.
It is the right, e'en of the lowliest,
To look up to the loftiest and to love.
As we may gaze upon the brightest star,
And have it back with kindly beams return
Our loving gaze.   Love is as worship then.

*The Princess and Paul go back and dance.   Mark and Julian come
    forward, Firing of cannon heard in the distance.*

Julian.   What sound was that?
Mark.   It was a cannon's roar.

Enter an Officer.

Officer.   The King is coming!
Julian   Ha! the King!
Officer. Those guns you hear do herald his approach.
A most disastrous battle has been fought,
In which our troops were routed utterly.
The King for refuge to the city flies.   [found my plans.
    Julian (aside.)   The King comes back! This will con-
But yet perhaps it is as well.   There are
More ways than one to Rome.   Napoleon turned
The Alps and then he scaled them and the Goths
Found paths for all their multitudes.
The King's a mad old tyrant, but he's vain
And can be flattered.   Flattery's the oil,
To lubricate these rusty natures with,
And make the human mechanism work,
With all its wheels and crooks and creaky cranks,
As smooth as running waters.   I'll go forth
At once to meet him, and I will contrive
To get his eye on me, and then with arts
And flatteries—for I will study well
To serve his passions and his vanity—
I'll steal my cunning way into his heart,
And make of him my tool, with which to win
Riches and power and sweeter still, revenge.
                                    Exit Julian.

Shouts heard without " The King! The King!"

Princess.   My father coming!   I must go to him.

*Exit Princess. The shouting and firing outside increase.   Great com-
    motion and confusion among the guests.   The curtain falls.*

ACT II.—SCENE I.

In the Palace. Enter PAUL *and the* PRINCESS.

Paul. To rule is God's prerogative ; and they,
Who under Him are rulers, e'er shonld be
Pre-eminent in god-like qualities ;
In goodness, wisdom, nobleness and truth.
The King should be the kingliest of men.   [realm ?
    Princess. If thou wert King how would'st thou rule the
    Paul. So as most to promote. throughout my realm,
Beauty and blessedness. I'd think me how
Heaven is, and I would seek to copy it
Among my people. Mansions beautiful,
For all the millions, midst sweet fields, should lift
Their towers and domes majestic to the skies.
The walls, around its cities, should be peace;
It's armies Liberty and Loyalty ;
And their bright armor, Justice and the Right,
And over them the banner should be Love.
And everywhere the people should be reared
Up to their perfect manhood : thus alike
Into the true divine similitude,
In which in Eden, beautiful they stood—
Not the poor growth of vice and ignorance,
But glorious in full developement ;
Each fit to be a king,—supreme in that,
The kingliest of kingly attributes,
The essential quality of the true King,
The power and habit of self government,
And thence through self control, pure thoughts just deeds,
Sole title unto power, sole right divine,
Fit to bear sway and rule by serving realms.
And woman beauteous, with man should stand,
Companion, peer, his mate, his other self;
Each to the other supplement in that

Sole perfect whole, true dual unity,
In which, the likeness of their Maker, erst
They stood, when He the universal parent,
Mother alike as Father of all life,
Created man in His own image, male
And female, counterpart thus of Himself.
And Beauty, artist of the skies, should come
With the lost plans of Eden and replant
Its gardens and its pleasant trees o'er earth
And make the fields as heavenly landscapes are.
With blossoms should it deck the bowers of love ;
And with sweet fruits fill all the abodes of peace.
Princess. It would indeed be glory so to reign.
Paul. It will be thine to win that glory yet.
Princess. I'll strive to win it. Wilt thou not assist
With aid and counsel, when the time shall come,
In these high aims ?
    Paul.   Ah ! would I were a Hercules,
With strength like his, to toil for thee, as thou
Should'st bid in every generous work, to add
Unto thy glory and thy people's good.
Princess. As partner in the work I'd have thine aid,
As counsellor and guide. I'll see you soon
Again upon this theme.
    Paul.   Heaven aid your grace !
                               Exit Paul.
Princess. Oh ! do I wrong to love him ? It must be
That Heaven intends it. From the first my heart
Sprang to him. I believe it, Heaven did send
Him unto me in its high purposes.
So stately and so wise, he's as I've dreamed
Of blessed beings in the upper world.
Give him a golden harp and he might stand,
As one amidst the bright and choral band.
                             Exit Princess.

ACT II.—SCENE II.

A Moonlight night. A Street in front of the Dwelling of Dr. John.
Enter FRANK.

Frank. It is all dark. I see a glimmer there,
As if there were a light burning within.
I'll try a song. Perhaps she will come out.

(*He sings.*)

Wake! Lady! Wake! fair is the night.
   There's not a cloud obscures the sky;
And in her stately beauty bright,
   The queenly moon doth walk on high:
Oh! Lady! come thou forth, that she
An equal loveliness may see.

Oh, come! the gentle breeze its tale
   Is whispering to the listening grove,
And the enamored nightingale
   Is pouring forth its lay of love.
Then come with me and tones more sweet,
A tale more true thine ears shall greet.

The light doth move. There's some one stirring there.
Another verse I'll try and then she'll come.

We'll wander in the moonlight fair.
   The stars shall witness from above
While in thine ear shall breathe the prayer,
   The prayer that's only breathed by love.
To win the answer sweet from thee,
The love that's more than life to me.

A noise! She comes! A brighter starlight now
Will beam from out her eyes upon the night.
Ha! Who is this? Her father! Jupiter

For Hebe! He doth see me not. I'll stand
Behind this tree and wait until he's gone.

Enter Dr. John.

[a dream.

Dr. John. There's no one here. It must have been
'Twas that Greek chorus running in my head.
I fell asleep repeating it. It still
Wrought in my brain and did suggest the dream.
Methought a choir, with flowers all garlanded,
Of those, who fought at Salamis, did come
With Sophocles for leader and did sing,
With harp and dance, peans of victory.
Such as I trust our youth will sing ere long.
The music flowed so sweetly, I would fain
Dream ever so, sleeping and waking too.
I think I can recall it. It began
Loudly, with a full burst and then it sank
To a soft strain. So. There. No. It is gone.
I almost had it. May not that be it?

Singing heard at a distance.

It is some reveller. 'Tis not the voice,
And all unlike the strange sweet melody.
It must have been all dream. Yet it doth seem
I heard it still, after I waked, although
Unto a softer sweeter strain it sank,
Just as, methinks, Apollo, when he'd turn
From Pallas unto Venus, with his lyre,
Would softlier sing. Well, well, I'll to my bed
And con the chorus o'er again. Perhaps
'Twill come to me once more in some sweet dream.

Exit Dr. John.

Frank. Greek chorus! Peans of victory!
Ha, Ha. Dear good old Plato! My poor song
Has waked in his great brain strains grand
And visions beautiful, as whispers soft,
Will in cathedrals and in galleries vast,
Oft swell and roll in loud reverberations.
She's coming now!

Enter Anna *from the house.*

Dear Anna! Darling! Thanks!

Anna. Dear, dearest Frank !

Frank. Forgive me for the sleep
I have disturbed and all the pleasant dreams,
I've put to flight. Not mine, but yours the fault,
In that you've made me love and long to come
And be thus ever with you, by your side.

Anna. More welcome is thy coming unto me,
Than sweetest sleep, or brightest dream could be.

Frank. As sweet to meet, so hard it is to part.
Oh ! tell me, when shall be the happy time
When there shall be no parting ; when all mine
Thou'lt be, I thine, each other's evermore,
Till death shall part us. When shall be that time ?

Anna. When thou hast triumphed in thy great attempt
To win our country's freedom, it shall be.
Then I'll be thine, thine only, wholly thine.
Then too, I'll proudly claim thee for mine own,
My husband, lover and my hero too.
But until then our country's must thou be.
She needs thee now and all thy energies.
'Twere treason to divert a thought from her.
When she is free, how proud I'll be of her,
And of thee too, her brave deliverer.
But said'st thou not, the club would meet to night
And that you must be there, to act with them ?

Frank. It does this very night. I'm on my way.
Matters of deep import we'll then decide.
And I am hastening to be there in time
But could not help but stop as I passed by. [man,

Anna. Ah ! would that Heaven had made me too a
That I might go with you to share in all
Your noble thoughts and plans for liberty,
And our dear country. Gladly would I go,
To toil and win or suffer by your side.

Frank. Nay, dearest ! Not to be a man. We then
Had never loved. Thou canst not wish for that.
Not for what's best in the wide universe,
Would I be otherwise than as I am,
Thus loving and thus loved by thee. No, not
With Michael would I exchange, to take
His radiant nature, with his place before
The seraphim and lose thy love and mine

For thee.

Anna.   True, Frank ! I do not, could not wish,
To be aught otherwise, than as I am
To thee, except to be nearer and dearer.
Not less but more would I be unto thee.
I more would share thy plans, thy thoughts, thy life,
Thy purposes of good, thy noble deeds,
Thy toils and perils in our country's cause.
Why may not woman strive and work and live
Aye, die too for her country ?   Must the paths
Of duty, peril and of honor e'er
Be trod by man alone ?   There'll be no sex
In Heaven !   May not we too nobly live
Our lives and leave bright records here, that we
Like you may look back proudly to them there ?
I'd e'er be woman, dear ! and be thy love,
But woman worthy of thy love, I'd be ;
A heroine for a hero ; by thy side
In toil and peril, as in love and ease,
To walk with thee in every path of life,
Partner in all thy labors, as thy joys.   [be.

Frank.   Such partner hast thou been. Such shalt thou
From thee first came to me these noble thoughts.
The inspiration was my love for thee,
And thy love my ambition and reward,
Thou dost and thou shalt share in all my thoughts,
Co-worker, with me in each generous aim.
Woman is ever man's true help and guide,
Her heart to him the best interpreter
Of duty and of honor.   Side by side
In work and love should they e'er walk through life.
But time doth fly.   I must now go.   I'll come
To-morrow and advise with you, of what
Is done and what should next be done, to aid
In our great aims for liberty.   I'll call
For Paul upon my way and will appeal
To him to join in our conspiracy.
Talk to your father.   Shape his mind aright.
In gentle words breathe noble sentiments.
And with your smiles scatter great thoughts around,
That they like coals of fire, dropped in the souls
Of men, may kindle into high resolves

And burst forth into deeds of nobleness.
The welfare of her country and the world
Is unto woman of as deep concern,
As it is unto man, and 'tis to her,
E'en as to him a duty and a right,
To labor for the general good,—for all
That tends to elevate our common race,
And beautify the earth, our common home.

Exeunt.

ACT II.—SCENE III.

Same night.   Before Paul's house.

Enter Paul and Frank.

Paul. Look at that star, yon lone one there, and think
How infinite the reach of its pale beam,
Traveling to us from its bright sphere so far.
So is it with our life and influence.
The truth we do, or utter goeth forth,
A beam of light and loseth not its way,
Amidst remotest centuries.
Frank.   Aye ! even so.
Paul.   The tree bears not it sweet fruits for itself ;
But 'tis that we may pluck and eat of it.
And so with golden fruitage of good deeds
And gentle influence should our lives abound,
To make the world more happy.
Frank.   'Tis most true.
Paul.   They the true artists are, who, as their days
Are given them, do mould them into lives
Of beauty ; and he greatest artist is,
Who makes his life the one most beautiful.
To live life rightly is the true high art,
The highest art, and to aspire in it
Is better, than to copy Raphaels.
Greater into a hero or a God
To mould one's self, than carve one out of marble.
Even Athos, hewn into his image, yet
Were poor to that which Alexander was.
They only truly live, who, with high aims
And noble deeds, do make their lives

'Thus real, earnest, true and beautiful.   [ours be.
   Frank. Aye, such should all life be. Such should
'Tis with such thoughts and aims I come to you.
There is a noble work, an enterprise,
The grandest sir! in which man can engage,
Than which earth has no better, loftier one,
Before us now. It doth appeal to us.
It craves the aid, it doth demand the aid
Of all good men and brave, and doth require
The highest attributes of mind and soul.
Tell me, dost thou not love thy country? sir!
   Paul. My country? If I know my heart I do.
   Frank. I know thou dost and therefore do I come,
Trusting to you. Hast thou not marked, alas!
The ruin that doth overspread the land?
Has not the general cry of misery
Pierced in thy ears and harrowed up thy soul?
Dost thou not see, that this once happy land,
By Heaven made so lovely, by man cursed,
Is prey to outrage, crime and misery?
   Paul. Alas! it is too true.
   Frank.   Why is it so?
Must it thus ever be?
   Paul.   'Tis clear 'tis not
Heaven's purpose towards us, for there's given us
All elements and means of happiness,
If men would use and order them aright.
   Frank. It is that tyranny doth crush the land.
The King is but a vile and hoary tyrant.
I'st not so?
   Paul.   Alas! it is too true.
Ah! why does Heaven so lavish power on them,
The coarse the vulgar souled, who cannot see
Its true and noble uses?
   Frank.   Strange is it?
Ha, sir! a muddle is it? muddle all!
Yet, sir! there's order in the way, the stars
Are set in Heaven, though they seem strown there
So wildly. Aye! and music they do make,
Could we but hear it, as they there do roll
In their eternal course. Heaven is all right.
'Twill do its part, if we do ours. Let us

Arouse and do our duty ; all will then
Come right and we will gain our liberty
And make our country free and happy yet.   [King ?
    Paul. What would'st thou do ? Would'st thou resist the·
    Frank. Aye, would I so,—resist his tyranny.
Shall we yield tamely, ever to these wrongs,
And with base acquiescence sanction them ?
Heaven forbid ! Submission unto wrong
Is treason to the right.   True loyalty
Is e'er a rebel against tyranny.
The despot is his country's bitterest foe,
And with him the true patriot can hold
No terms but those of strife and enmity.
With tongue, and pen, and sword and dagger too,
'Tis his to battle against tyranny,
And toil, and plot and fight for liberty.
    Paul. Alas ! What can we do ? What force have we·
To battle with the tyrant's brutal troops ?
    Frank. At least sir, we can do our best,
And serve our country with what force we have.
The right is mightier than armies are.
Let's do our duty, and in doing that,
We will achieve the truest, best success ;
For duty done is ever victory.
What though 'tis difficult.and perilous !
Were there no mountains we would never climb,
And danger as a bride the brave man loves ;
For there's in her a beauty and a charm
To fascinate and win souls of high strain ;
And honor and renown are born of her,
From each encounter some fair child of fame.
Let's do our duty, and as you just taught,
Live truly in high aims and noble deeds,
And make our lives thus great and beautiful.
Aye, aye, sir ! The life beautiful ! Ha ! ha !
The hero and the god ! I have you there ,
By your own words I have you.   He, the Paul
Of old, whose name you bear, not only taught
The good fight, but he fought it too,
And by that name, and its great memories,
His cross, his crown, and your own noble words,
I do appeal to you to join with us

In this great work, to win our liberty
And make our dear, beloved country free.
   Paul. For our dear country and for liberty !
You need make no appeal to me for them.
I am, and ever was, and will be all
For our poor country and sweet liberty.
Show me but where the path of duty lies,
In which to serve them truly, and I'll tread
It gladly, fearlessly, though perils, toils
And agonies assail at every step,
And death itself, confront me at the end.
Here is my hand ; I'm with you, sir, in this ;
For life and death, I'm yours in this just work ;
But tell me of your plans and purposes,
The steps by which you seek to reach these ends,
And realize these glorious results.
   Frank. A company of students, all your friends,
Have joined in secret, sworn conspiracy,
Vowed to achieve our country's liberty.
We are thy comrades all, and love thee, sir!
And wish to have you with us at our head ;
Our chief to lead us in the ways of glory.
Wilt thou not join us in our sacred vows ?
   Paul. Aye, any place in the great work I'll take.
But tell me of your plans, the special means,
By which you seek to realize your aims.
   Frank. Come with me now. We meet this very night.
In the old ruined abbey, in the church,
A wild, lone place, off in the royal chase,
Just at the forest's edge, where none will come.
The peasants tell that spirits rise at night
And flit amid the trees and through the tombs
And broken vaults, and wander till the morn.
There secretly and safely we can meet.
Our brother Angelo will meet with us.
He is a spirit medium, as you know,
A rare, pure soul ; one of those wondrous men
Who have appeared in these, our later days,
Successors to the seers of olden times.
Of nature delicate, yet powerful,
He seems to have some strange affinity,
Some power o'er spirits, that they're drawn to him,

And through him will communicate with men,
And speak of matters of the other world,
Things future and invisible.   He'll come
And sit in council with us, and through him
We will receive celestial utterances.
And we can ask the spirits of the dead,
Of the old heroes, who in ages past
Have fought for liberty, to come to us
With help and counsel in our glorious work.
Come with me.   'Tis at one o'clock we meet;
And see! the broad-faced moon, now at its full,
And swinging in the vault right opposite
The sun, is passing the meridian,
Marking midnight to us, as Phœbus doth
Midday to the antipodes.   Come, sir!
Mark now is waiting with the President.
Let's haste.   We'll help him carry it along;
And I'll explain to you as we do go,
More fully all our plans and purposes.
 Paul,   I'll go with you and see what I shall see.
 Frank.   The sky is changing.   There's a storm at hand,
I never hear that whistle in the wind,
That sad, peculiar, melancholy moan,
But that I know a storm is on the wing.
Exeunt.

ACT II.—SCENE IV.

Same Night—A park on the edge of a forest.   Enter FRANK, PAUL *and*
 MARK, *with the skeleton enveloped in a mantle.*

 Frank.   'Tis heavier than I thought.   Let's stop and rest.
There.   Stand it so.
 Paul.   He's like a reveller,
All masked and mantled for a masquerade.
How far is't to the abbey?
 Frank.   Yonder, there
Above the forest rises the old tower.
How spectral-like it stands against the sky!
 Mark.   You're right, sir!   Cæsarism's bad enough,
Even with Cæsar's glory gilding it;

But with the Neros and the little Cæsars,
It is a pure, unmitigated curse.
    Frank. With nothing to redeem it.
    Paul.   A sham too,—
Poor Cæsar's mantle, as in it he fell,
E'en at the base of Pompey's statua,
And which should have been buried with him then,
But which usurpers steal to ape in it
His vanity and crimes and that—without
His genius and his generous, grander traits.
    Frank. It is the same old fable of the ass
In the lion's skin, made true and realized
In history.
    Mark. With a refreshing change
And variation of the character
Of brute, exhibiting in that old skin ;
Fox, wolf, bear, hog and calf, and now and then,
In its capacity for shedding blood,
A specimen of genuine leonine.   [quick
    Paul. How strange it seems. If men were wise, how
Would fall the Cæsars and the Juggernauts.
    Frank. Have you heard of the history I've writ ?
    Mark. What you ? No. History of what ?
    Frank.   I have it here.
'Tis this. 'Twill do to read by moonlight.

He reads.

An ass found a dead lion's skin.
With wring and twist he crept therein,
He shook the mane, he reared the tail,
While all the beasts around did quail.
At length a bear did cross his way ;
At him the ass a roar did bray.
The bear, no bastard bear was he,
Rushed at the ass right bearishly,
From off him stripped the imperial skin,
And straightway in his place crept in.

    Paul. Ha, ha ! What name give you your history ?
    Frank. The sequel to " Thiers' empire."
    Paul.   Aye ! 'Tis apt.
The sequel to yours, I should like to see.

Frank.   May hap you may :—wait a decade or so.

Mark.   Come sir ! Now prophesy. How long think you
This old imperial skin will last. to serve
These bears and asses thus to fool men with ?

Frank.   Well, 'tis a tough old hide.   It has endured
Some nineteen centuries.   And sir ! the blood
That they, who've aped the imperial brute in it,
Have caused to flow, is as a river is
Unto a rivulet, to what has served
To slake the thirst of all the genuine brutes
That through these centuries have raged o'er earth.
A tough old hide, but cracked and rotten now.
'Tis in its twentieth century, but 'twill
Not last it out.   If you do, you will see
The end of it.   That is my prophesy.
Hist ! Who comes there ?

Mark.   'Tis Julian.   Mark his stealthy gait !

Frank,   He has a certain look, that answers pat
To my idea of Judas.

Paul.   It is said
That he has won the favor of the king.

Frank.   By flattery he wins the tyrant's ear.

Mark.   He's shrewd and cunning.

Frank.   Aye, mere cunning, sir !
And cunning is but wisdom's counterfeit ;
A poor and shallow one.   He's hollow, false,
And lacks the true, substantial qualities.

Paul.   Falsehood is ever shallow, hollow, null.
Truth only is substantial, solid, sure.
Dishonesty is ever a mistake.
The lack of honesty is lack of sense,
Of due perception of the scope of things,
Of their relations and true harmonies,
And just adjustment of act to the fact.
The rascal ever is a fool, at least
To the extent of his rascality.
And hence I rather pity him than blame,
And in the treatment of the criminal,
I ever with the prison would combine
The school and hospital.

Frank.   Hist ! Here he comes.
The clouds sweep o'er the moon ! He'll see us not.

A cloud passes over the moon. Enter JULIAN, not seeing them.

[right and wrong.]
Julian.   'Tis wrong Ha! Tut! Mere names these,
Virtue! Pooh! 'Tis mere talk,—a name devised,—
An artificial sentimental sweet,
To sugar o'er tame deeds to weakly souls.
That's right to me, that rightly serves my will,
And that is wrong, that thwarts me ;—that's my creed :
The true one for a resolute brave soul.
Of universal being, 'tis the law,
Each atom to itself all else to draw,
Itself the centre of the universe.

The cloud passes from the moon.

Ha! who is here ?
Frank.   Good evening, sir !   [is this
Julian. Ha! Frank! and Mark! and Paul! and who
That stands with you, so stiff and statuelike,
Mantled and masked in such strange mystery ?
Frank. Nay, sir! You see he doth disguise himself.
Wisdom prics not in what concerns it not :
Of its own proper food it heaps its store ;
And like a thrifty husbandman it digs
In its own field.
Julian.   'Tis guilt and cowardice,
That mask themselves and lurk round in the dark.
Frank. Ha, Ha! Is that the view you take of it ?
Well, sir! this is a face that need not mask
Its beauty from the moon. Nor fear nor shame
Can start a blush in it. Look! Is it not
An open and an honest countenance ?

He draws the mantle from the skeleton.

Julian, (starting back.) Ha! Horrors! How it star-
tled me, so hideous.
Mark. Ha, Ha! I thought you had more nerve in you.
Julian. Who would not start to have thus sprung on him
Such image of grim death grinning at him ?
Frank.   'Tis but the counterpart of your own self.
We're all but skeletons with skin o'er them,
That like this mantle will some day drop off
And nothing leave of us but bones, mere bones.

You might as well thus tremble when you look
Into your glass.   Look sharply there, you'll see
This same queer compilation of white bones,
And that same ghastly grin will mock at you.
Tut, sir ! you're frightened merely at yourself.
But we must haste.   Come Mark ! Let us march on.
Good night, sir !

Exeunt Frank, Mark and Paul with skeleton.

Julian.   Good evening, sirs !
Curse them.   They laugh and jeer at me.   Well let
Them have their jest.   I'll have mine too ere long,
And echo back their laughter at them yet.
But what means this ?   There is some mystery here.
There's something up, when skeletons do walk.
Mystery's the cloak, that mischief ever wears
To do its dark work in.   I'll hie with this
Unto the King and set the spies on them.
Already I'm his favorite.   I'd stake
My life against a butterfly's, that I
Could bend him unto any whim I'd choose,
So that it be some vain and wicked thing.
He's doubtless an old tyrant, a mere beast,
Drunken and brutish, and his tyranny
Rests fearfully upon the realm.   These wars
He madly wages and his cruelties
Do make him hated, and the citizens
Are ripe for insurrection, and do nurse
Imaginings and dreams of liberty.
E'en now their leaders do in council meet,
And I have pledged myself to meet with them ;
And would do so, but suddenly the King
Thus fancies me, and through him best I see
My way unto my own peculiar aims.
Hence I'll at once reveal to him their plots.
'Twill be a new and double treachery.
But doubly 'twill secure my hold on him :
He, who connives at and accepts a crime,
As guilty is as he, who does the deed.
As partner doth he thus commit himself
Both in the crime and to the criminal.
The briber doth as truly sell himself,

His honor, manhood and true dignity,
As he who seeks and takes the filthy fee.
In buying me, to serve his tyranny,
The King too sells himself to me, to serve
My aims both of ambition and revenge.
There's strife and trouble brewing in the state,
But 'tis midst tempests the true sailor's shown ;
And in these rough wild times, the bold and shrewd
Win their best prizes.   I have heard it said
That where hell boils the hottest, there the waves
Were molten gold.   So here, the roughest times
Throw richest treasures up for those, who know
And dare to seize them.   I will venture it
That in the general pillage and turmoil,
I will secure my full share of the spoil.

Exit.

ACT II.—SCENE V.

Same Night—A large Gothic Church, partly in ruins, dimly lighted in front, the rear beyond in darkness.   The Club assembled.   The Skeleton in the chair.   Present: PAUL, FRANK, ANGELO, MARK, ERNEST *and other Students.*

[hour,
Frank. Brothers ! the hour's at hand, the wished for
Such as Columbia saw at Bunker Hill,
And Greece beheld of old at Marathon,
When for our country we may draw our swords
And fearless strike for her and liberty.
Our prayer is answered.   The glad hour is near.
Soon from its scabbard every blade must leap,
Ne'er to return till victory replace
It back, with dints of glory all emblazed.
Then comrades ! let us seize the golden chance
With hearts exulting and a gallant blow
Strike for our country and sweet liberty.
Let us now solemnly renew our vows,
That in the coming crisis we will prove,
In all our duty to the fatherland,
Most firm and faithful.   With uplifted hands,
Let us most solemnly swear this to Heaven.
All.   We swear it.   We swear it.   We swear it.

Paul. Let's sing ere we do part. Some good old hymn.
Frank. What shall it be ?
Mark.   The Marseillaise !
The strain most eloquent of earth and time.   [score,
  Ernest. Nay, "Scots wha hae" let's sing, the brave old
That rang at Bannockburn.
  Paul. Old Hundred ! Luther's grand old air, let's sing.
Several voices. Old Hundred ! Old Hundred !
Frank. Old Hundred let it be. All join in it.
Sing ye, as David and as Luther did,
And as they would, if they were with us now.

They sing the doxology to Old Hundred.

Mark. Now for the spirits—'Tis the hour for them.
  Frank. Ere we do part we'll sit awhile to learn,
What revelations from the spirit world
Will be imparted to us. Our good friend,
Through whom these mystic voices speak to us,
Is delicate of structure and his frame
So sensitive and finely strung, it yields
To every airy influence and thrills
Accordantly, if but a spirit comes
And waves his wing, or breathes a whisper near.
And as the future to the spirit's ken
Is as the present visible and clear
We may some intimation haply get
Of what fate has in store for us, in these
Most perilous times, or else perchance we'll hear
Some word of heavenly counsel, that may teach
Us how to serve our country. All take seats.

Enter a Sentry.

Sentry. A storm is gathering. Ye had best make haste.
The roaring of the forest, where it comes,
Is as the voice of ocean in a storm.
'Twill soon be here. 'Twill be a fearful night.
  Frank. If there's to be a tempest, it is like
The spirits will be out in fuller force.
'Tis said, they love the wild winds and the storm,
And joy to mingle with the elements,
When they in mad career sweep o'er the earth.
  Angelo. Around the table we will all take seats.

They seat themselves around the table.

Paul. These spirit revelations of our day
Do make the old-time faiths seem probable
That taught of airy shapes and forms of light,
The fair divinities of air and sea,
And nymphs that haunted mountain, grove and stream.
  Angelo. They show, that round about us in the air,
Spirits are hovering ever near to us,
Familiar loving friends, and ministers
To do us service, fleet as sunbeams are.
They hear our voices, bear our messages
Unto our loved ones in the world unseen,
Spy out the secret thoughts of men, and from
The pages of the future read to us.
Let us with pure intent and honest faith
Invoke their gentle presence, and they'll come
And o'er us shed celestial influence.
And with that spirit vision, that doth pierce
Through time and space, will show to us the way,
Where victory waits us with sweet liberty.
Let us in patience and in humble faith,
Accept the signs and words vouchsafed to us.
Upon the table all around join hands.

They place their hands one on the other around the table.

There is a world within this outer world,
A realm unseen amidst this visible one,
Of essence all too subtle for the grasp
Of our coarse senses. Its bright habitants,
Etherial beings, disembodied souls,
Hovering in robes of airy textures, wove
Of paradisal hues and gleams of heaven,
Are all pure spirit. They have wings and limbs
Like thought, agile to pass from star to star
When they go out in space, on errands bent
Of love or duty, or when off they range
The illimitable regions, to explore
New realms unseen before of worlds and wonders.
Oft in excursions out they go, far off
Into the deep,—amidst the stardust fields,
Or, where, beyond in the abyss, light droops

Its wearied wing amid the vast extent,
Lost in the trackless, shoreless infinite,
To make discoveries, of what God there
Has reared of beautiful, in the drear void,
And what of life He's breathed to dwell in it
And make it the abode of love and joy.
'Tis their delight thus to go forth and roam
Amidst His worlds, to study out His laws,
And solve the mysteries of His providence.
For 'tis the business of the spirit life,
In which with sweet employ they fill the years
Of the eternal ages, thus to search
His works and find out all His ways, and more
And more to know, the more they learn of Him,
That all his ways are good, and all his works
But Infinite Love wrought out by Infinite Power.

    Mark.   Hark ! Hush ! What sound is that ?
    Ernest.   It was a cry.
    Paul.   Out in the forest!
    Mark.   No, 'twas in the tower.
    Ernest. To me it seemed, as if it 'twere from beneath.
    Frank. Aye, there the monks are buried in the vaults.
That yonder is the statue of a knight,
Who fought in Palestine and then turned monk.
His tomb is there beneath the monument.
Near to him lies an old inquisitor ;
And then a saint of such dread sanctity,
That at his word the fiends would baffled flee.
    Mark. The peasants say that strange unearthly sounds
Do linger round these ruins in the night;
That spirits in the breeze do sigh and moan,
And often shrieks are heard upon the winds
And yells and howlings most unnatural.
    Ernest.   Ha ! There's a sound.
    Frank.   It is a rap.
    Ernest.   There, there. Now hear them, how distinct.
    Angelo.   Some spirit comes.
    Mark.   I trust it is a good one.
An evil spirit in this fearful place,
And at this hour might do us injury.
    Frank. Now hear it rap. It rattles quite a tune.
A trill of spirit-land. I hope 'twill speak.

Angelo.   Is there a spirit here would speak to us ?
Frank.   Three raps it makes, answer affirmative.
Lo ! see ! the table moves ! It rises up !

The table rises and moves about in the air.

Ernest.   This is most strange !
Mark.   Most wonderful !   How can it be ?
Paul.   By signs and wonders Heaven in ages past
Was wont to intimate its will to men.
Frank.   'Tis like the air is full of spirits round,
That look on us, though we may not on them,
And hence this wondrous seeming miracle.
Angelo.   There's more within our vision, than is in
Our vision.   Spaces infinite stretch out
Within our very reach and ages glide
In every moment.   In these depths of time
And space, wonders exist we dream not of :
Armies, that Xerxes could not number, throng
Around unseen, and compass us about
With glittering legions and great deeds are wrought,
That would make fields renowned, and written out
Fill libraries of history.
Paul.   It settles back again unto the floor,
How gently !   There, it upwards moves again.
It seems as if with spirit 'twere instinct,
Or else that spirits round did lift it up.   [world
Frank.   'Tis thought by some, that this our visible
Is mere illusion, an ideal show,
Some action of etherial attributes,
Of the same essence, as is thought or spirit.
That spirit the true substance is, more real
Than what we guess of and do matter call ;
As life not death is the reality.
Atoms of force not matter people space ;
Monads of soul, minims of melody,
Living and loving agents, from whose play
And workings into ceaseless harmonies,
These glories visible and those unseen,
All unimaginably glorious,
Is this our wondrous beauteous universe ;
One infinite eternal symphony.
Ernest.   The table now rests quiet in its place.

The Skeleton moves.

[move.

Frank.   Look! there! See there! The skeleton doth
Haply 'tis our departed brother.   He
Perchance doth stir these bones, knowing they're his,
As when in life he walked in them.   I'll speak
To it.   Art thou our brother's spirit?
Mark.   There were three raps, distinct ones.   It is he.
I hope he'll answer and converse with us.
Paul.   See Angelo,—his eyes are fixed—he seems
As in a trance.   What may his motions mean?
He acts as he were writing.
Frank.   Haply thus
The spirit would communicate with us.
Let's give him paper, and see what he'll do.

*He places paper before Angelo and a pencil in his hand.   Angelo
writes and Frank reads.*

I am your brother's spirit.   It is still
My privilege to meet with you and share
Your hopes and counsels.   When high thoughts
Are whispered to your souls, then know that I
Am hovering near to you.   I now am here
To rouse you up to noble purposes.
There come with me three mighty souls, that wrought
Of old for liberty and who would still
In spirit aid the cause they loved in life.
Hark ye unto their words and make
Their deeds and lives the pattern of your own.
Ernest.   This gives us blest assurance, that our friends
Departed hover yet in spirit near
To us, and that we too may after death
Still linger in these dear accustomed scenes,
And mingle though unseen with those we love.
Frank.   Mark Angelo! His eyes are closed, and look!
A strange far light seems breaking o'er his face;
A glorified expression, as it were;
As if a gleam from Heaven did shine o'er it,
Or as some soul beatified had come,
Or spirit blest and waked in him the thoughts
And raptures of the invisible world.

His aspect is as if inspired and rapt.

Mark.   Hush ! He will speak to us,   The spirit now
Struggles in him laboring for utterance.

Angelo.   I sang erewhile of war in Heaven ; of Sin
And Evil vanquished, and their rebel hosts
Hurled headlong hideous into the abyss.
Sublimest theme too, for celestial song;
Oft chosen by those other bards, minstrels
Who fought upon the fields, of which they sing,
Mighty alike with sword or harp.   Crowned now
In silent shades and seats embowered they sit,
Deep pondering the eternal chronicles,
And of them building heavenly Iliads.
Oft held in stillest rapture, Heaven doth hush,
With all its multitudes, entranced to hear
Those sweet seraphic voices chanting deeds,
By sword of angel and arch-angel wrought,
Or arm of the Omnipotent.   The war
Is but transferred, to be fought out on earth.
The same bright armies, Powers of light who fought
Those fields in Heaven, with the old ensigns still,
And armor from celestial armories,
And decked with Honor's true insignia,
The scars of battles fought for God and truth,
Legions that faithful ever stood, still stand
In arms embattled 'gainst the Powers of Hell,
To drive them forth from earth as erst from Heaven.
With them are leagued all who love God and good,
The true and wise of earth, the spirits pure,
The just and generous ones, who are for Peace
And Liberty and God's eternal truth.
The contest on the earth is supplement
And counterpart to that renowned in Heaven,
And deeds are done heroic, that will vie
With aught wrought by the sword of Michael
And be fit themes for loftiest minstrelsy.

Ernest.   He sinks exhausted back into his seat.
The spirit or mysterious energy,
Whate'er it be, is passing from him now.   [earth's

Frank.   'Twas Milton's spirit.   He, who sang the
Sublimest strain.   His was the loftiest soul
Of England's noblest age.   He in his life

Did ever speak and act for liberty.
Paul. The song he sang he still can sing in Heaven.

Noise of wind and storm heard without.

                                    [now.
Ernest. Hush! hear the tempest! It has reached us
How fierce it strikes and dashes 'gainst the walls.
    Frank. The old tower reels, but braces up again.
'Twill stand as it has stood a thousand storms.
See! He doth rise. 'Tis like he'll speak again.

Angelo rises.

    Mark. Another spirit now doth enter him;
He's all unconscious. How his form dilates,
As if some mighty soul expanded it!
With what a calm and stately majesty,
He looks yet sees us not. There's that in him
In look and attitude, like what we note,
In statues that we see of Washington,
Who it is said was of a lofty mien,
An awe compelling presence.
    Paul.   Can it be
His spirit? Art thou he, who was in life
The mightiest champion of liberty,
And dost thou still in spirit sympathize
With those, who in thy steps would carry on
The work thou didst begin so gloriously?
There, see! his lips do stir. He'll speak to us.
A word from him were as a voice from Heaven.
    Angelo. The loftiest path of glory is where treads
The patriot fighting for liberty,—
To make his country happy, free and great.
Such is the path, in which 'tis yours to tread.
Heaven marks it out for you; your country calls,
Duty commands, and Honor becks you on.
The spirits of old heroes, who have fought
For freedom hover with me o'er you now,
And bid you emulate their noble deeds.
Numbers innumerable, shining hosts,
With banners waving that have waved o'er scenes
Renowned—in shadowy troops, as erst they marched
Upon the battle fields of liberty,—

'They come from hillside old, and storied plain,
And holy haunted vale, where fallen they
Have lain sleeping in glory. Be ye true.
Victory will yet be yours and proud renown.
The millions of the free will bless your names.
Armies invisible will fight for you ;
And Heaven send swift legions to your aid.
   Paul. He takes his seat. Can it be so ? Is this
Illusion, or the trick of vile imposture ?
Or was't the soul of Washington, that spake
In him ? I would believe it was. 'Twould give
Assurance that our cause is blessed of Heaven,
And that success will surely follow it.
Lo ! see ! Is that a vision ? Angels armed !
The heavenly armies now are marching here.

*A flash of lightning lightens the church and figures of Angels, &c.,
are seen on the walls.*

   Frank. 'Tis Michael and his angels in pursuit
Of the rebellious hosts, that routed fly
Smote by avenging thunders. I've oft come
And gazed at the grand figures on the walls,
Though marred by time and ruin, beauteous still.
It was the lightning flashing through the church,
That made them visible. There, 'tis again.

Lightning and thunder, &c.

That leading angel seemed to lift his sword
And strike with it as the flash fell on him.
   Mark. How deep the thunder, as it rolls along !
   Ernest. The rattling of His chariot through the skies!
   Frank. The old church trembles to its very base.
There's not been such a storm, since that wild night,
The cross on the cathedral spire fell down.
The priests then said, it was the devils work.
There, lo ! The glorious vision comes again.

Lightning and thunder, &c.

   Paul. Horses and chariots of fire of old
Did fill the mountains round the man of God.
The same God liveth with His armies still;
And hosts with chariots flaming and bright arms

Of heavenliest temper, proved in ceaseless fights
With hell's fierce legions, are encamped around
On every height, to aid His champions
And with sure reinforcement give them help
In every righteous cause.
    Mark.   Hist! He prepares to speak to us again.
He rises! There's frown upon his brow
This is a spirit of a different sort.
    Frank.   There is a haughty grandeur in his mien,
Like to a statued Roman.   See!   He moves
His arm, as he would wrap a robe around him,
And as he trod the seven hilled city still.
He grasps that dagger, as he knew its use.
    Angelo.   'Tis right to fight a tyrant any way,
With sword or dagger, or in peace or war,
In open strife, or dark conspiracy.
The tyrant and usurper have no rights.
They trample upon every law and right.
With them there's none, for them there should be none.
There was a dagger once, that freed the world
From an usurper; the earth's loftiest one;
The foremost man of all the world, my friend
And lover: but he wronged my country and
I slew him.   Take this weapon:—rightly used,
It will work out thy country's liberty.
Be bold and use it as a patriot should;
As Brutus would, were he alive and this
His country; the old Rome that he so loved.

He hands the dagger to Paul.

    Frank.   It was the noble Brutus, he who slew
Cæsar Imperator.   'Twere well had we
A spirit of his mettle living now.
    Mark.   He pointed out the shortest, surest way,
For our deliverance.   Would some strong arm
Ensheath the dagger in the tyrant's heart,
The work at once were done and we were free.
    Frank.   By handing so the weapon unto Paul,
He seemed to mark him out, as the right one
To do the work, and strike the glorious blow.
See him!   How on the dagger he doth gaze,
And then on empty air and all enrapt!

Paul.   Why did he give this weapon unto me?
That I should use it on the King, as he
Of old did upon Cæsar?   I kill him!
I an assassin!   No, oh! no, not I.
I'll draw my sword and wield it in fair fight,
And in all just and honorable ways
I'll give my life up to my country.   But
A murderer I may not be.   Not that!
Heaven! point me not that way; but any path
Of peril or of sacrifice mark out,
To drain my life out drop by drop for her,
Or toil 'midst pain and utmost agonies,
And I will tread it gladly, fearlessly.
But I assassin may not, cannot be.   [the steel
    Ernest.   No, friends! Not such our course.   Not with
Of the assassin, but the soldier's blade,
Must our great work be wrought.   In open war
We will encounter him, and boldly drag
The tyrant from his throne.   Such is the course
Doubtless that Heaven intends us to pursue.
    Paul.   Then wherefore dost it send to us such signs
Such dread and solemn messages?   Why is't
These tables move, and the dumb elements,
With eloquent action, thus appeal to us,
And spirits of the dead, who in their graves,
Have slept for centuries, now thus come forth
And intimate to us these fearful deeds?
Is it thy meaning Heaven?

                Lightning and thunder, &c.

                            Is that thy answer!
    Mark.   In the old days of signs and prodigies,
Thunder was deemed to be Heaven's voice to earth.
    Ernest.   A crashing peal!   'tis a most fearful night.
The powers of the air are out in arms,
With Heaven's heaviest artillery,
And every one with lightnings in his grasp.
A fiercer tempest never shook the hills.
'Twill test our bravery to encounter it.

                A signal heard.

    Frank.   It is the signal.   There is danger near.

The sentry gives the alarm.   We must away.

Enter the Sentinel.

                                [trayed !

Sentinel.   Away ! Quick for your lives !   We are be-
A troop of soldiers now are marching here.
  Ernest.   I see in this the serpent traitor's trail—
Sir Julian we must thank and pay for this.
  Frank.   Out with the lights.   Take up the skeleton,
And follow me.   I know a secret way ;
A subterranean passage though the vaults,
And out into the forest neath the walls.
Thence we'll escape.   The tempest is our friend.
Heaven for our safety thus doth interpose.
Amidst its thunders and wild roaring winds
Our steps will be unheard, and its thick veil
Will cover us and hide our swift retreat.

                            Exeunt omnes.

ACT III.—SCENE I.

In the City.   Enter PAUL *alone.*

  Paul.   Ah ! wherefore will that dagger haunt my mind,
And never leave me ?   Still 'tis there—'tis there.
And the old Roman's words ring in my ears,
And startle fearful echoes in my soul.
Aye, more, my country seems to plead to me.
How blessed it would be, were he to die !
Then gentle Peace would reign, where now this fiend
Of blood doth ravage.   Ho ! thou kingly Death !
Thou, who art cursed so oft by gentlest souls,
For laying low the lovely and the good,
Thou now could'st win for thee unnumbered thanks
From all the hearts of this wide realm, if thou
Would'st on this tyrant do thy blessed work.
Would that the spirit of old Rome walked still.
The noblest citizen of all should rise
And arm himself and slay him and there's not
An honest heart in all the world but would
Exult in it and bless the righteous blow.
Shall I then kill him ?   Shall I strike that blow ?

It were to do my country a great good.
It were to take one vile pernicious life,
And by it save a thousand nobler ones.
Aye! shall I kill him? I! oh! no. I kill?
Whose dreams have ever been of light and love
And beauty? Shall I stain my soul with blood?
Away from me, thou hideous fearful thought!

Enter MARK, ERNEST *and* ANGELO, *with Students and Citizens armed*

Mark.   The people rise in insurrection. Hear
The cannon's roar! The city's in revolt!
And foremost in the tumult, shouting march
The students, singing hymns to liberty.
Come Paul! join with us, if you freedom love.
                                        Exeunt all but Paul.
Paul.   How little is our life in our own hands
To shape it as we wish. A drama 'tis,
Writ by another, we the players merely.
My heart's fond aspiration e'er has been,
To live a life pure, beautiful, like Christ's,
Devoted to some high and noble aim,
Some mission of bright love and gentle Peace.
But destiny doth will it otherwise.
And hence the path, that nearest it, I'll take,
The path trodden by Washington.
I'll fight for freedom ; for my country I
Will work, that I may give her liberty.
Yet rather were not my true course the one
That Brutus chose? 'Twere more effectual sure,
And rightly viewed perhaps as glorious.

Enter FRANK *and* ANNA.

                                                          [on!
Frank.   Come, Paul! come with us ! Gird your **armor**
The city has revolted from the King.
He's thrown our good old Master Dr. John
Into the castle dungeon, heaped with chains,
Thence to the scaffold to be dragged and hung.
This outrage stirs the people to revolt.
Now is the time to drag the tyrant down.
Paul.   Alas ! our dear old teacher? What's his **crime ?**

Anna. The crime of which the wolves accuse the lambs;
Which fiends against the seraphs ever charge,
And guilt 'gainst innocence. Goodness is e'er
An accusation and offense to sin,
And wickedness may truly see in it
Its bitterest and sternest enemy.
This is my father's sole yet fatal crime.
 Paul. Upon the scaffold to be hung you say?
 Frank. Yes, by to-morrow morning's earliest hour.
At sunrise on the castle's highest tower.
 Paul. Can there be nothing done for them? *him*
 Frank.   There will.
We'll storm the castle ere that hour,
And o'er our bodies, heaped against the walls,
Climb to the rescue up the battlements.
Hear you those bells? Mark you these cries around?
It is the city rising in revolt.
 Anna. The people roused and arming for the fight;
And with them at their head the students march.
 Frank. Yes, they do swear with solemn oaths to yield
Never unto the tyrant's sway again.
Thou'dst have exulted to have seen the crowd,
The high hearts of the city, bare their heads
And all together lift their hands to Heaven,
And swear they would be free. It was a sight,
To make old earth laugh in its rocky ribs.
Then at the name of Liberty, a shout
Went up to Heaven and forth they marched with cries
And hymns of triumph through the exultant streets.
 Anna. And foremost, at their head the students
   marched—
Thy gallant comrades, they with whom so oft
Lessons of glory thou hast learned, and pored
O'er deeds for freedom wrought by heroes old.
 Paul. The King! How does he act?
 Frank.   Fierce as a butcher. He
Is leaguing with the neighboring tyrants round.
E'en now a hostile army marching threats
The city. The scared despots from all sides
Will rush to trample out the holy fire
Of liberty.

Citizen.   Alas! Alas! Ill news
I bring. The citizens have fled. A troop
Of students fighting, who refused to fly,
With Angelo, your comrade, at their head
Were taken prisoners. The King enraged
With fearful blasphemies swears they shall die.
     Anna. Can you stand calmly cold and hear all this?
     Frank. A leader we do need. Wilt thou refuse
To be our captain and to lead us in
The ways of glory?
     Paul.   Cold! calmly! Oh, No!
Could I by laying down my life for her
Save my poor country, gladly would I die.   [say.
     Anna. Die! no. 'Tis live and fight, that you should
'Tis not your death but life, true earnest life
And action bold and prompt in her behalf,
That now your country needs and asks of you.   [yield
     Frank. What would'st thou have us do? Must we e'er
In soulless tame submission, to these wrongs,
These deep accumulated, crushing wrongs,
That tyranny may please to heap on us.
May right ne'er arm itself 'gainst brutal wrong?
May never sweet, sweet liberty be ours?
And wilt thou bid us rear our children slaves?
     Paul. I bid thee? No, I say not so. Not mine
To counsel peace with tyranny. I scorn
The man that can rest quiet in a land
Trampled by an oppressor. Never I
Will bid the sons of freedom pause,
In their march onward, while of earth a foot
Is trodden by a despot. No! while floats
A rag of the black flag of Slavery,
Let never Liberty ensheath her sword,
But ever be sleepless and armed for battle.
Doubt me not! I'm all thine and Liberty's.
     Frank. There spake our noble brother. Arm thyself,
Thou art our captain. Lead us where thou wilt
We'll falter not, though death bestride the path.

Enter a Citizen.

[rallied.

Citizen. Good news! Good news! The citizens have
With barricades they hold the troops at bay.
And bid defiance to them.
   Frank.   Huzza! huzza!
Let's haste to them! Unto the barricades!
There take our stand for victory or death.
Come, Paul? Wilt thou not go with us?   [elsewhere.
   Paul. Would that I could––but Heaven now points
Go you at once unto the barricades.
Withstand the tyrant's troops until the morn.
Before the dawning I will come to you.
Till then there's work for me elsewhere to do;
By which haply to serve our country well;
A duty that Heaven doth impose on me;
A path that I must seek and tread alone.
Go now. I'll follow soon. Before the morn
I'll join you at the barricades and march
With you to storm the Castle at your head.
   Frank. So be it then. We'll to the barricades,
And hold them with our lives until you come.
                    Exeunt all but Paul.

   Paul. It is the way—the way. The King should die.
My comrades plead to me to save their lives,
My country calls, Justice demands the blow.
His death alone will serve. While he doth live,
There is no hope of peace. Nothing but blood
And tyranny and riot through the realm.
But were he dead, sweet Peace would smile again,
And hope and calm security and joy
Like sudden sunshine lighten up the land.
Shall I then kill him? That's the point, my soul!
To stain with blood thy purity and all
Thy dreams of beauty to dispel, by that
Vision of horror, which once seen, will haunt
Thee ever! That's the question, oh my soul!
That Heaven puts to thee, and thou must answer it.
Heaven! meanest thou that I should do this deed?
Why else dost thou suggest these thoughts and make
That which has ever been so horrible

And criminal now seem a solemn duty !
I'll go first to the palace, to the King,
And with the gentle Princess, who I know
Will join with me, I'll strive and plead with him.
If that avail not, then—such other way,
As Heaven shall in its justice point me to.

                                            Exit.

ACT III.—SCENE II.

In the Palace.   Enter the PRINCE *and* PAULINE.

Pauline. How many of the students have been taken?
Prince. A score of them ; all brave and gallant youth.
The King declares he'll hang them every one.
Pauline. Alas! and can there nought be done for them?
Can there be found no inlet to his soul ?
No spot that we may touch of human mould ?
Take me to him.   I'll plead and beg for them.
Perhaps sweet pity's fountain, in some vein,
Deep in his stony nature, hidden sleeps;
If we can pierce the rock, it may gush forth.
Prince. 'Twill need some power like that of Moses'rod,
To smite the rock in him effectually.
But what can will be done.   The Princess now,
And Paul with her, is pleading for their lives.
Pauline. Heaven help them plead and touch his heart.
Prince.   Amen.
There comes his tool and flatterer.   Let's go.
                        Exeunt and enter Julian.

Julian.   The Princess interceding with the King
For mercy to these rebels ! and with her
Her saintly lover ! Ha, Ha! It is strange,
That flower so sweet should spring from rock so rude.
Not beauty, sir ! nor intellectual gifts,
Nor love, nor prayer will stir his brutal soul.
Besides I'll ply him with the drink he loves,
That he relent not, till they're out the way.
And then I'll plot to send Paul after them,
And then the insurrection in the state
Once quelled by force, and the King's sway confirmed,

Why I, who by my arts and flattery
Do rule the King, through him will rule the realm.
They come.

Enter the KING, PRINCESS, PAUL, The PRINCE, PAULINE, *Officers and others.*

 Princess. Wilt thou not spare them for my sake ?
 King. No, ask me not. I've sworn that they shall die.
 Princess. Father ! my birthday on the morrow comes.
A princely gift then thou hast promised me.
Give me their lives. I'll prize the present more,
Than if you'd heap before me gems and gold—
All rarest pearls, rubies and diamonds bright,
The spoil of Orient treasuries, and all,
That e'er were gathered in earth's hollow halls,
Grottoes and caverns vast, where Genii dwelt
In the primeval ages, and with them
Illumed their stately domes and decked their thrones,
Or if the wealth of California's streams
And the far isles of the Pacific seas
You'd give to me the dowry of thy love. [dews.
 Julian. Seraphs have bathed her lips with heavenly
All puissant is Beauty with her tears.
Tears are the drops to wear the rock away.
 King. Not all that wealth, were it thrice ten times told
And piled here a ransom at my feet,
Would buy their lives or save them from my wrath.
 Paul. May't please you, sire! Grant me to speak a word.
'Tis good to have power, glorious, Godlike power,
That we may use it like God, for good ends.
'Tis glorious for the imperial sun
To sweep through space upon its shining way,
With its bright train of glad attending worlds ;
And oh ! 'tis good for us that the grand orb
Doth sway the earth and in its blessed path
Amidst the starry fields lead her careering ;
For ever with its beams come light and life
And beauty to our else poor dreary world ;
And all the myriad golden rays it sends
Are busy ministers of good to us,
Angels of loving sweet beneficence. *e/*
And so should they be, to whom power is given,

Mighty as is the orb, but with that might
Tempered by love and mercy, e'en as God,
Who gives that power, holds His omnipotence
Subservient to His goodness and His love.
    Julian. Hist! hist! He's preaching to the King.
    King.   Ha! how?
    Paul. Forgiveness is the noble soul's revenge,
The sweet redress the generous spirit craves.
It is the justice that the just exact,
E'en as they'd have that justice dealt to them.
'Tis ever wisdom's truest policy.
'Tis sweeter, as 'tis nobler than revenge;
It plants a keener sting than vengeance can,
And works a more effectual punishment.
It vanquishes the guilt it punishes,
Subduing it to love and gratitude.
Revenge doth but repeat the very wrong,
It would redress. Its spirit is of hell,
Malignant, cruel, blind with hate, it most
Upon itself doth wreak itself, like hell,
Its own chief victim. But sweet mercy is
The highest, heavenliest attribute of Heaven,
And in the fullness of its own rich peace,
It doth return of its abounding joy,
Kindness and good even for injury.
How blessed—
    Julian. Jehu and Jehoshaphat!
He'd made a grand old prophet. 'Twas just so
They used to come and chide the old Jew Kings.
    King. Ha! Silence! Where are kept the prisoners?
    Officer. They wait in chains your majesty's commands.
    King. Take them at once to execution. Hang   '
Them all forthwith. Thou hast thy answer. Hast
Thou more to say?
    Paul.   No more—to say.   [not send
    Princess. Oh! give them time for prayer. You would
Them unprepared to their eternal doom.
Give them a space to fit their souls by prayer
And ministry of holy men for death.
Oh! for my sake, thy daughter's, grant them this.
    King. Till midnight then I'll give them. At that hour
Let the great bell be tolled. Then have them strung

Around the outer battlements, that there
Traitors may see the doom that waits for them.
Now for a brave old revel.   Give me wine.

They pour out wine to him.

I love to see bright wine, rich ruby wine,
The purple blood of the red grape—but more
The redder richer gore, that traitors pour.
    Pauline.   If there is blood in him, it must be black.
    Prince.   'Twere just, if he were by hyenas torn,
Or trod upon by elephants and crushed
Out of the form of the humanity
He doth disgrace.

Enter an Officer.

    King.   How now ? sir, speak !
Thy smiling doth bespeak for us good news,
As a bright dawn doth herald a fair day.
    Officer.   Most happy news.   The citizens do yield
And flee behind the barricades.   The troops
Are gathering swift and hem them round.   As swoop
The eagles from their flight upon their prey
We'll charge on them and take them prisoners.
    King, (giving him a ring.)
Take this, sir ! for your tidings.   Now haste back,
Hedge them around that none escape.   We'll drain
Each drop of rebel blood from out the realm.
To clear a land of reptiles 'tis the way,
Each viper, soon as found to crush and slay.
Now for a right brave revelry to-night.
Pleasure shall speed the moments in their flight.

        Exeunt all but Paul.

    Paul.   Heavenly Justice ! What are thy thunders for,
That they do roll so vainly through the skies
And blast him not ?   Monster insatiate !
Right wert thou, Brutus !   Wert thou living now
There'd be a deed more noble to be done,
Even than that brave blow, which gave thee fame.
There should be in each land some officer,
Some righteous man, whose office it should be
To slay these tyrants, who abusing power,
God's attribute, do use it thus like devils.
I'll rush in now and stab him where he stands.

Ha! shade of Brutus! comest thou again
With thy red dagger, smiling as in scorn
That thus irresolute and weak I halt,
Scared by these scruples, fears and timid doubts,
Shadows perchance, unreal as thou art?

Enter Princess *and* Pauline.

Pauline. Alone here? brother! What is't aileth thee?
There's pain and anguish written on thy face!
What is it that thou gazest so upon?
There's nought that I can see but the bare wall.
See'st thou some vision in the empty air?
Paul. Dost thou see nothing? Then there nothing is.
Pain! no! Sweet sister! Wrong! It were not wrong.
There'd be no guilt in it. 'Twere right and noble.
Pain! no. I have no pain. 'Tis duty calls. [dering,
Pauline. Thou heed'st us not. Thy thoughts are wan-
And fixed thy gaze. What is it? Speak to us.
Paul. It should be done, yet oh! not I, not I!
Princess. It should be done! What is it should be done
Not thou! 'Tis duty calls! What dost thou mean?
Some fearful thought absorbs thy mind. Speak, sir,
Thy Princess and thy sister bid thee speak.
Paul. Harmonia child of Mars! Aye, even so.
From fiercest discord sweetest harmony.
Thy mother was some angel lost on earth,
Some daughter of the skies, loved by thy sire,
And hence hast thou thy peerless attributes.
Princess. My father—
Paul. Thine, thy father—that is it.
Princess. Forgive him. He is old and passionate.
These troubles in the state have maddened him.
He will relent—A brighter day will dawn,
And in the hope of it let us await,
And from the future borrow happy thoughts,
To cheer the gloomy present. Let us hope.
                              Exeunt Princess and Pauline.
Paul. It's right? Have I the right? Admit, he is
Unfit to live and by his crimes deserves
To die, can I take rightfully his life?
It is a question. And yet, why is not
That right in man, which wrought by God, in Him

Were good and blessed ?   So the aim be pure,
And the result be good, the deed the same,
What matters it by whom or how 'tis done ?
This life of ours, this strength, even our wills
Are all from Him.   In us they e'er should be
And are as still incorporate in Him.
Our thoughts and acts are not our own, but His,
In whom we live and move and have our being.
Hence we should ever, at each turn of life,
Imagine to ourselves, what thought or deed
Would become Him and fearless then we should
Do it exultingly.   And there's no act
However dread it be, but it, so done,
Is good in us and Godlike, even as if
'Twere wrought by His right hand.   Would it not then
Be a most blessed deed, if God would take
This tyrant from the earth ?   Then why not too
If I should do it ?   Or, rather He through me,
I, even as the dagger in my hand,
So I in His merely an instrument ?
I'll with this question go once more to Heaven ;
And if unto my mind, looking to God,
It still seems right, I'll take it at His will,
His working in my soul and pause no more.

He leans his face against a pillar.   Enter JULIAN.

   Julian.   Ha ! Paul !   Weeping is he or praying ? I
Could now dispatch him.   No, 'tis not the time.
I will not mar my plans by hastning them.   *Exit Julian.*
   Paul.   'Tis so.   'Tis right.   So says the voice within.
And to each man the voice of his own soul
Is God's own special oracle.
'Twere cowardice in me if I should pause,
Scared by this dim vague phantom, we call "wrong,"
While thus my country calls and pleads to me.
And in my thought, to serve my country, it
Were nobler on my soul to take the guilt,
If guilt it be and bear its penalty,
Aye, peril if need be body and soul,
And sacrifice for country, earth and Heaven,
Than shrink from fear of it.   My country ! thine
The blessing—mine the guilt and punishment.   [*Exit.*

ACT IV.—SCENE I.

Night—In the Palace.   Enter PAUL *and* PAULINE

                           [speak ?

Pauline.   She leaned upon your arm while you did
Paul.   She did.
Pauline.   And smiled ?
Paul.   Yes as a seraph might.
Pauline.   Were you alone with her ?
Paul.   Yes, quite alone.
Pauline.   What was it that she answered unto you ?
Paul. 'Twas less in words than looks, that she replied.
It was her glance and that sweet smile, that played
Upon her lips.
Pauline.   Was that all ?
Paul.   All.
Pauline.   Oh ! Fie.
You should have urged your suit to her, have clasped
Her hand and bent your knee and from your heart
With the full fervor of true earnest love
Have plead and prayed to her till she did speak
And answer back to you with love for love.
Paul.   Nay, nay, my sister !
Pauline.   Yes, yes, my brother ! Never tell me nay.
Paul. You do forget her rank.   A Princess she.
The daughter of a hundred sceptered kings.
Pauline.   A Princess !   'True, but she is woman too.
In love she's but a girl, a simple girl.
Is royalty, think you all void of soul ?
May Princes have no hearts for love and joy ?
Love ! 'Tis the highest honor Kings can win,
And the best homage we can pay to them.
Love laughs at titles and the toys of rank.
Nature doth rank us as we stand compared,
In stature and in quality of soul.
Your heart will mate you with their royalest
Aye, you, my brother ! more do honor her
By the rich offering of your pure high love
Than she could honor you, were she to place
The crowns of all her sires upon your brow.

And if, as I believe she love, 'twill be
Her joy, her pride to heap upon you all
Her princely powers and high imperial honors.
But I must haste. Good night. May slumbers sweet
And dreams of love be thine.

Exit ~~Princess.~~ Pauline

    Paul.   Heaven guard my sister!
Can it be so? It is so. She is right,
Now that I think her words and actions o'er.
'Tis strange I saw it not before. Her love!
Oh! could I clasp her in my arms, 'twould be
Of Heaven more, than Heaven itself could be.
Aye, what could mean those words she spake to me?
How would I rule the realm, if I were King.
What should that mean? And then—would I assist
With aid and counsel when the time should come.
Aye, when the time should come. 'Tis so. Aid thee,
Sweet Princess? Yes, the treasures of my youth,
All that I am and all I hope to be,
The energies of the immortal mind,
The might of love, these passions and high thoughts,
All I'll devote unto thy service. Yet. No.
Dreaming of love with murder in my heart!
To love the daughter and yet slay the sire!
Away, ye dreams! No, not for me is love,
Or hope, or sweet delights. Stern duty bids;
Heaven has commissioned me; my country calls;
It is my mission and I must not fail.

Enter the PRINCESS and THE PRINCE.

[come

    Prince. I like not these fierce cries and shouts, that
From out the city. There's new trouble there.
I will go forth to learn what it may be.

Exit the Prince.

    Princess. Why is it thou art thoughtful? Lo! look up!
Diana there is out, with all her troop,
Her starry nymphs, hunting in the fields of Heaven.
Is it not beautiful?
    Paul.   Most beautiful!
    Princess. This loveliness, that robes the night,
Suggests to me a thousand happy thoughts.

Tell me. of all created things that are,
Which most would'st thou delight to be ?
 Paul. Of all created things ?
 Princess.   Yes, let it be
Something whose nature we could share with thee.
 Paul. Then thou shalt guess it. Thus I will find out
What thou would'st wish to be and that I'll wish.
 . *Princess.* It is a star thou'dst be ; a Pleiad there—
One of those walking yonder. Would'st thou not ?
I'd fain be one of them—dost thou not think
The stars are conscious of their lofty life ?
 Paul. Aye, do I so. I would not, could not deem
Those glancing orbs mere dead and senseless things.
To me the universe is all alive,
Instinct with soul and sense and thought and joy ;
And Nature doth delight in all her works,
Even with a joy infinite as her might.
And these her wondrous movements thrill her frame,
As when great thoughts move o'er the soul of man.
Yet I'd not be a star. There's that to do
Upon the earth, I would not leave undone,
Not for the brightest of yon golden seats.
 Princess. Is it a cherub then, that thou would'st be,
Or seraph with thy home in Heaven, and thence
Oft times to go out, visiting amidst
Yon shining worlds, a messenger of light
On holy errands ? Thou could'st then come back
Unto thy native earth, to do thy works
Of love and mercy.
 Paul.   Nay, not yet, not yet,
There's a time coming, when I hope to be
Such seraph, haply then to dwell near thee,
In some sweet nook of Heaven, but not yet.
 Princess. Then tell ; what it is thou would'st wish.
 Paul.   It is
That I could be awhile omnipotent,
With power to execute on earth, what I
Would love to do. There'd be a change here then.
For I have thoughts of beauty in my soul,
That wrought out would make earth all glorious,
As if with jasper walls and gates all pearl
And golden pavements built it cities were.

The elements of glory all are here;
Richest material for the new Heaven.
The marbles waiting lie beneath the hills,
Yet crop out looking round for architects.
How easy, if men would, 'twould be, to rear
Them into palaces. Ah! were men wise,
This world might be all beauty, life all joy.
The hills with burnished domes would gleam afar ;
The valleys all would happy valleys be,
And all the isles be islands of the blest.
    Princess, I wish thou could'st have such omnipotence.
Enter the Prince and an Officer of the Palace.

    Prince. The insurrection in the city spreads.
They seem to march this way. I fear their plan
Is to attack the palace and thus aim
The blow they strike at the most vital part.
    Officer. With fiercer blow we'll meet and parry it—
Our guns will give them greeting as they come.
Enter a Servant.

    Servant. The mob is marching hither and their cry
Is " To the Palace"—"Death unto the King." [troops.
    Princess. Heaven help us, should they overpower the
    Servant. Or should the soldiers fraternize with them,
And join the work of pillage and of blood.
    Princess. Alas! Is there such danger ? Then indeed
To Heaven must we look. (*To Paul*) You will not leave us
The people love you. They will heed your voice,
Better than armor or of brass or steel
Is the bright panoply that Love puts on.
I choose you as my knight, to watch for me
And guard me through the perils of this night.
    Paul. Unto thy safety will I give my life.
    Officer. The shouting seems to cease and die away.
    Princess. Perhaps the tumult now will quiet down
And all be well. Keep ye good watch   Good-night.
                    Exit Princess.
    Prince. Where is the King ?
    Officer.   Dead in a drunken sleep,
They brought him senseless from the night's debauch.
The trump of doom could not awaken him.
He lies in yonder chamber. That's the door.

Paul. Ha ! Did'st thou mean to point the way to me ?
Prince. Hark ! Hear those cries again ? Let us go out
And learn what they do mean.   Paul ! you remain,
We'll soon return and make report and then
Council of war together we will hold.
The gentle Princess doth rely on you.
    Paul. So,   Heaven is working it.
    Officer.   Heaven working it ?
'Tis Hell you mean.   It must be thence that comes
The inspiration, that impels these fiends.
Hark, hear them yell !   A legion at the least
Is busy now at some devil's work, devised
For them in hell.   Watch you till we return.
The Princess' room is next unto the King's.
Keep you near there.   She may require your aid.
The King's not like to wake or trouble you.
    Paul. 'Tis very likely that he will sleep well.
                        Exeunt all but Paul.
'Tis clearly Heaven's appointment.   It is so.
It is a duty.   It is more than right.
It is a duty.   It will be an act,
In the esteem of thoughtful just souled men,
Noble and righteous.   Good men will approve
Of it and history, if it ~~right~~ *write* true,
Will put it down among its purest deeds.
In killing him 'twill be but one life lost,
And that a criminal's, by every crime
Polluted and by every law condemned.
While by it lives unnumbered will be saved,
Lives which may beautiful and happy be.
Thus too the Princess I can best protect,
For were he dead, I could at once go forth
Unto the people and proclaim his death ;
It would disarm their rage and turn their hearts
Again to her in love and loyalty.
And all at once through the now mourning land
There would be peace and sweet security.
My dagger, come !   Thou'lt yet a relic be.
I'll pause no more, but to the deed at once.
               Exit Paul and enter Julian.
                          [ger thus,
  Julian. What may that mean ?   He grasped his dag-

Sternly as if he'd strike with it.   I've seen
Him oft of late buried in reverie ;
Then he would start—and gaze into the air,
Then clench his hand and mutter to himself,
And drop and shake his head, all lost in thought,
As if he meditated some dread deed,
Some fearful purpose.   I will dog his steps,
And play the spy on him.   When saints do arm,
Then rogues and devils well may take alarm.

Exit.

ACT IV.—SCENE II.

Night.—A street in the city barricaded—Ernest, Students and Citizens
armed, some on guard, others sleeping, &c., &c.

Citizen.   What cries are these that come upon the breeze?
Ernest.   It is some tumult in the city.   But
That we must stay to man the barricade,
I would go forth to learn what it may be.
Citizen.   From different points do come the sounds,
Shouting and roar of guns, and with the breeze,
Billows of music swell upon the ear.
Ernest.   'Tis a new rising of the citizens.
They've waited for the night to arm themselves ;
And now they march with shouts and songs in bands
To join the insurrection.
Citizen.   Look there, to the east !
How red the day-break lightens up the sky.
Ernest.   Nay.   Midnight has not struck.   It is the glare
Of conflagration.   The city is a fire.
See how those flames curl round yon eastern tower,
As if hell from beneath were bursting forth.
They seem to lick the skies with their forked tongues.
The night doth linger long.   Would it were day.
These fearful scenes will fright the morn away.

Shouts and singing heard in the distance.

[here
Citizen.   Hark ! They are jubilant.   They're marching
With cries and hymns.
Ernest.   How hollow sounds the earth
Beneath their measured tread.   There's thunder in

The tramping of the people, when they arm
Themselves and onward march for liberty.
Let's wake our sleeping comrades, and as they
Do come, give them a fitting welcome.   Friends !
Awake ! Halloo ! Rouse up ! awake ! Halloo !
The citizens in troops of thousands come.
A myriad swords leap from their sheaths to-night
To strike for freedom.   Wake ! halloo ! halloo !
    Citizen.   It is some solemn death chant that they sing.
How grandly rolls the chorus on the air
In the still night.   They bring their slain with them.

Enter Mark with a troop of students, &c., bearing a dead body.

    Mark.   Comrades ! fall in the ranks and march with us !
The city everywhere doth rise and pour
Its eager thousands to our aid.   Onward !
Unto the palace we will march t'avenge
Our murdered friend and win the liberty
For which he died.   All fall into the ranks !
Unto the palace, onward ! on, march, on !
    Ernest.   Who is it that has fallen, whose remains
You thus do bear with you, with such display
Of triumph and of woe ?
    Mark.   Alas ! 'Tis Frank.
The brightest spirit of us all has flown.
    Ernest.   What, Frank ! our noble, genial comrade gone.
Keen wit, warm heart, true friend and generous soul.
Dead is he ? dead! alas ! How did he fall ?
The brightest Pleiad now indeed has fled.
    Mark.   His death was worthy of him.   At our head
Upon the barricade he stood and back
Repelled the rushing soldiers, and in turn
Did chase them fleeing, and with cheers
Urged the pursuit.   Even as he fell, he waved
His sword above him, shouting " victory."
His last words, as we raised him, were, " I'm free."
He smiled, and 'twas the same bright smile we've seen
So oft, and then his spirit sprang away,
To join the freed ones in the immortal realms.
    Ernest.   I'll join them too with him ere morn and day
Shall dawn on me in Heaven, if we win not

Our liberty. Aye, liberty or death !
That is our word—our battle cry.
Onward, march on. Freedom and victory !
  Mark. We must be on the march, Let all fall in.
The tyrant in his stronghold we will seek.
The wild beast in his lair, and from his den
Drag out the monster. To the palace, ho !
Take up the body. Bear it at our head.
That is his fitting place, to lead us still
Until the victory. On to the palace !
We'll sing as we do march. On ! Forward, march !
                              Exeunt, all singing.

        Hark ! from the skies, a voice that cries,
        There is no nobler death or prize,
        Than his who for his country dies,
            Fighting for liberty.

        Carry him proudly to his grave ;
        Around him still the true, the brave;
        The flag he loved above him wave,
            The banner of the free.

        Waste not for him or sigh or tear,
        Above him lift the exultant cheer,
        For his the fate to hero dear,
            Martyr of liberty.

        Like his may be our destiny,
        Like him to live, like him to die,
        Like his, the graves where we shall lie,
            And his, our eulogy.

ACT IV.—SCENE III.

In the King's Bed Chamber. The King in his bed. Enter PAUL.

  Paul. The way is clear ; yet I would rather creep
The vast earth round, than walk this little space
Unto this deed. Where is my dagger ?

He draws a Dagger and with it a manuscript from his bosom.

I've writ my reasons here for what I do,
That should they kill me, as most like they will,
They'll see I acted in it righteously.
And chiefly that the Princess thus may know
Why I did slay her sire and that she may
Be more induced by it to rule the realm
In love and righteousness and gentle peace.
And haply too earth's tyrants thus may learn
Elsewhere that justice may awake for them.
How innocent thou look'st, dread instrument!
Blood may be wiped from thee, but will its stain
E'er leave the soul?   I'll think no more of it,
But to the work at once.   Yet first I'll kneel
A moment, the last time perchance on earth,
And ope my heart and all its thoughts to Heaven.

He kneels, then soon starts up, dropping the manuscript.

Is it a troop of spirits that I see?
Or an illusion is't?   Bright beings there
Do hover o'er the King.   They beck to me.
Ye blessed messengers!   Is it to aid
Me in the bloody work, that ye do come?
Will ye receive his spirit in its flight?
I would not harm his soul, but for his crown
Of earth would give him a celestial one.
They're gone.   Was it illusion?   Am I mad?
Yet will I take it as a sign from Heaven.

He goes to the Bed.

How still he sleeps!   How pale and like to death!
Here is his heart.   'Tis here I'll strike.   Ha, no,
He breathes not.   Pale and still he lies.   'Tis death.
He's dead already—God has slain him.   Done
Himself his own just work.   Yet no, his breath
Returns—faintly, as if 'twould die away again,
As life were struggling feebly against death.
I thought that Heaven had saved me from this deed.
It still is to be done.   Yet scarce he breathes.
Death with a little help will do the work.
It stops again—perhaps he now is gone
And if I wait I may be saved the deed.

A Bell tolls.

The Castle bell! He bade it toll—their knell.
It is his too. It bids me haste to stop
These fearful murders and these hideous crimes.
I may not wait—He may revive—They'll come,
And then too late—I must now make it sure.
So. So. 'Tis the best way.

He smothers the King.

He struggled not !
And not a breath. Was he not dead before ?
I know not which has slain him God or I.
The deed whate'er and whosoe'er it be
Is now on record in the eternal books.
Let heavenly justice only credit me
With motives pure, such as did prompt the deed,
And with the countless blessings that will flow
From it and I'm content. I'm clearer now
In thought and conscience that the deed is done.
Hist! did not some one speak ? I thought I heard—
Ye spirits ! Is it ye still hovering round ?
I do believe that ye are near me now,
And that ye have been with me in this work,
And will bear witness of it unto Heaven.   *Exit.*

ACT IV.—SCENE IV.

Hall before the King's Chamber. Enter PAUL.

Paul. I never heard that Judith was condemned.
Nay, rather every age hath blessed her deed.
True, 'twas her country's foe, whom she did slay.
Yet to my mind the ruler who proves false
And doth oppress his country, or in wars
Involves her needlessly, more truly is
That country's enemy, and guiltier far,
Than any foreign hostile foe can be.

Enter The PRINCE, JULIAN, *Officer and Servants.*

Prince. Awake the King ! The citizens attack
The palace. Haste ! the mob is marching here.

Exeunt Officer and Servant into the King's Chamber.

Come, comrade ! Rouse thyself. There's work to do,

That we may save the Princess and the King.
The hydra-headed monster comes, the mob.
Oh ! for an arm and club Herculean !
    Paul.   A lyre and hand Orphean better were.

Enter Servant.

Servant.   The King is dead !
The Prince.   The King !
Julian.   Dead ?
Servant.   Dead in his bed, he lies.   [the guard !
Julian. Dead ! He has stabbed him then. Quick ! call
Here's the assassin.   Search and ye will find
The weapon on him, that he killed him with.
I do accuse him as the murderer.

Enter the Officer.

                                [stand ?
Prince.   Did'st thou not hear him?   Silent dost thou
He doth accuse thee and thou answerest not.
Can'st thou have dared to do this fearful deed ?
If so, to Heaven and to thy country's laws
Thou'lt have to answer it.
    Paul.   For what I've done
I'll answer to my country and to Heaven.   [still.
    Julian.   Search him !   Perhaps the dagger's on him
    Officer.   Nay, there's no wound, no blood upon the King
Nor mark of violence.   He's not been stabbed.
He lies as calm as if he'd gently slept
His life away.   It is the hand of God.
Our friend is here to watch at our request.
'Tis clearly God's own judgment, and in it
He has been His own executioner.
    Julian.   I'll go and see how 'twas he did the deed.
                Exit Julian into King's room.
    Prince.   Most like, 'twas in some sudden fit he died.
His spirit ever stormy has been set
In whirl in these wild times, and thus has flown.
Heaven in its purposes has taken him.
Forgive me, friend !   'Twas clearly God's own hand.
    Officer.   More like, he passed away in that deep sleep
In which we brought him from his revelry.
He drank too deep.   A deadly stupor 'twas,
He's never roused from it.   But hear these sounds

It is no time for lamentation now.
These cries demand an answer. We must act.
How would his spirit now have roused itself
For flght. Alas, old warrior! thou'lt wake
Unto the roar of battle never more.
   Prince. Act! Aye a mighty scene is opening now,
'Twill need great actors to perform it well.
Oh! for one fit to take the leading part,
A star, with genius for a general,—
Heaven's gift most precious, in it's hour of need
Unto a country, a good general!
Come, Paul! go with us. Canst thou not devise,
Some plan, some path to lead to victory?
   Paul. Thou leadest still! Thy hand still points me on!
I will obey you sire! I'll go with you,
To serve Heaven and our country and the Queen.
Let me go to the people. They will hear
My voice. The King's death I'll proclaim to them;
Then of the gentle Princess I will speak
And of her sweet and heavenly qualities.
And I will point them to the enemy
Before the walls and 'gainst them turn their rage,
That they with us and with the troops will march
To drive the invader routed from our soil.
We'll in the night go forth and seize the heights
About the foe and compass him around,
Then at the dawning we'll rush down on him
And strike him as with lightning out of Heaven.
   Prince. There wakes the hero. You're our leader sir!
The people love and they will follow you.
I do commission you, our general,
You've struck the path of glory the first stride.
Fame's wreathing now a chaplet for your brow:
Pegasus has come down and kneels to you
You've but to mount to be among the stars.

    Exeunt all, and then re-enter Julian with Paul's manuscript.

   Julian. No wound nor sign of violence. Yet—yet
I'm not content. There's some deep mystery here.
That dagger and his rapt and intent mood,
In which he rushed away—then here alone—

And the King dead—dead, in his bed.   It is
A mystery.   What's this I found?

He opens and reads the manuscript.

                      His writing!
I found it on the floor by the King's bed.
That shows that he was there.   What does it say?
" The King a tyrant!"   Ha! " the Princess Queen!"
Aye, that's the ladder by which he will climb.
" Gentle and loving!"   Hell! in love with him!
Curse him! I'd stab him were he here.   'Tis so.
It is argument to justify
The killing of the King.   This devil saint!
'Tis said the meekest spirits, when they fell,
Did make the fiercest devils.   It is so.
'Tis clear that he did meditate the deed.
It shows most plainly, 'tis proof positive,
He had it in his mind to kill the King,
And in some way by poison or foul means
He's wrought his purpose and has murdered him.
And all the same as murdered me ; my hopes
All blighted, dead in the King's death, while he
Will love and triumph.   In the Queen's love
What height is there to which he may not climb?
Yet, ha, I'll have him yet.   I will rush forth
And straight proclaim him as the murderer ;
She cannot love her father's murderer ;
And I'll so demonstrate his guilt to her,
That hate and horror from her heart will drive
A love so guilty and unnatural.
Yet no, not yet.   He'll have confederates.
The mob do love him and me they do hate.
If they should find me here, they'll wreak their wrath
And vengeance upon me.   I must away,
And hide until this riot has been quelled
And order is restored ; then will I come
And in this saintly lover of the Queen
I'll prove to her, her father's murderer.   *Exit.*

ACT V.—SCENE I.

*Street in front of the House of Dr. John. Daybreak—Anna at the
Window.*

Anna. 'Tis day—the light is breaking o'er the east;
The sun is rushing on and soon will rise
And give the signal for my father's death.
Oh! why is not Frank here? He promised me
To come or send me word before the dawn.
What if he's fallen in this fearful night!
My father murdered! My love slain! Ah me!
I would go forth, but where? And should he come,
And I away. He bade me stay. Be still
My heart—I can but wait. I must be calm.

She Sings.

Oh! it is sweet to be beloved,
And Oh! to love, 'tis sweet.

There comes a crowd. They're armed and pour along,
As if into a battle they did rush.
If he's with them, he'll make some sign to me.

Enter a crowd of Students and Citizens armed &c., &c.

[Haste, haste,
Officer. Hurrah! my men! Would we had wings.
Or too late for the battle we shall be,
And miss our portion in the victory.
A bulletin for him, who's bravest now!
Student. Heaven grant to us that we may be in time.
I would give years of ordinary life,
To be there in the hour of victory.
Citizen. Hurrah, Hurrah! On—On, We'll all be brave
And merit though we win not bulletins.
Merit is ever better than success,
And to deserve more than to win renown.
Exeunt.
Anna. He was not there. Most like he's gone before,
And now stands foremost in the stately ranks,
Where death is picking out the bravest ones.   [*Sings.*

Oh! it is sweet to be beloved,
    And oh! to love 'tis sweet.
But both to love and to be loved
    Is bliss indeed complete.
The light from eyes, that mutual shine
With loving looks, is light divine.

Ah me! singing at such a time!
Father and lover both gone; dead—or death
Perchance poising at them his fatal shaft—
I all alone! Would I could die with them.
'Twas the last song he sang to me—the last
Perhaps he'll ever sing. If so, the last
Too I will ever sing.—Ha! who is that?
My father? Father! Blessed Heaven! 'Tis he.

She rushes to the door. Enter Dr. John. She throws herself into his arms.

                                                [to you.
   Dr. John. My daughter! Heaven has brought me back
   Anna. 'Tis Heaven indeed has brought you back to me
For this is truly Heaven. How was it you escaped?
   Dr. John. The King is dead. The Princess, now our.
       Queen
Has thrown the prisons open. All are free.
   Anna. The Princess Queen! That is glad news indeed.
Gentle and loving will she ever be;
Her sway the same even ~~the same~~e as liberty—
Better if ruled by love, than to be free.
Aye, doubly bright the dawn that's breaking now.
   Dr John. The bright dawn ever follows the dark hours.
Let's ever cherish Patience and sweet Faith.
The earth rolls on—however black the night,
'Twill bring us out into the bright clear light.   [cries?
   Anna. But why these guns and shouts and fearful
Do they resist the Princess and refuse,
To yield unto her gentle blessed sway?
   Dr John. No. All rejoice to know that she will reign,
And with glad welcome hail her as their Queen.
But now without the walls a desperate fight
Is raging with the proud invading foe.
The citizens and troops together march
To drive the enemy from off our soil.

In desperate battle are they now engaged,
And this the din and roar of the fierce fight.　[Speak!
　Anna. Heaven be with them. How goes the battle?
Is there no word or sign how it inclines?
　Dr John. Nothing but what these noises do portend.
List to the distant sounds. There is a change;
The cannonading slackens and doth seem
To roll off in the distance, as the foe
Did yield before our army. Sounds it not
Fainter and farther to your ear? Hark! Hear!
　Anna. Fainter the volleys strike upon the ear,
And duller boom the echoes 'gainst the sky,
As if the battle farther rolled away.
Hist! I hear music! There it is again!
Do you not hear it? From afar it comes.
　Dr John. Nothing I hear but these fierce noises **round**
And the deep distant booming of the fight.
　Anna. Through all these sounds it pierces **to my ear;**
Nearer and clearer to me it doth come.
'Tis a triumphant strain—a peal of joy.
Do you not hear it? Clearer now it comes,
And there—a cry I hear. A shout far off;
A whisper as it seems. It comes again—
It is—it is the shout of victory.　　　　　　[true.
　Dr John. Heaven grant that it is so, that she hears
　Anna. Louder and higher rises that glad strain
And clearer ~~rise~~ the shouts upon my ear *ring*
And victory—victory is all the cry.

　　　Music and shouting heard in the distance.

　Dr John. I hear it now. 'Tis a triumphant peal,
And with it mingle cheers and cries of joy—
Shouts of glad tidings halloed from afar.

　　　Bells ring, cannon fired and shouting heard.

The city now is learning the glad news,
And pouring through the streets wild with delight.
Aye ring ye bells! be jubilant ye guns!
Let universal joy shout through the land!
　Anna. The Lord is with us—God is on our side.
He giveth unto us the victory.
He makes the right to triumph by His might,

And scattereth iu flight his enemies.
The foe doth flee ; the oppressor is no more ;
Our Country is redeemed and we are free.
The Lord be praised.   Let glory evermore
And thanks be paid unto His holy name.
   Dr John.   Most wonderful is our deliverance.
A great salvation has been wrought for us.
Had He sent forth His angels visibly
From Heaven to fight for us, His gracious help
And goodness unto us, in this our need,
Could not have been more plainly manifest.
Here come the people.   They are mad with joy.

Enter Citizens.

                         [here.
  1 *Cit.*   Huzza, Huzza !   They come !   They'll soon be
  2 *Cit.*   Yonder they are—there is a troop of them.
Here's the brave soldiers.   See how proud they march.
  3 *Cit.*   And well they may 'tis a proud day for them.
  4 *Cit.*   Aye ages hence they'll speak and sing of it.
  5 *Cit.*   A mighty hero general he'll be.
  1 *Cit.*   He could have taught old Boney tricks of war.
  2 *Cit.*   The greatest victory of the century.
  3 *Cit.*   The greatest since Charles beat the Saracens,
And slew a million of them in one day.
  4 *Cit.*   I wish he'd lead an army 'gainst the Turks
And rescue from them the Lord's sepulchre.
  2 *Cit.*   A million men would march with him for that.
  3 *Cit.*   I'd go with him.
  Sev. Cit.   And I, and I.   [with him.
  1 *Cit.*   Aye, all the boys who're brave would march
Here come they with the prisoners.   Huzza !

Enter Soldiers with Prisoners in procession.

   Dr John.   These are the fruits, the sad results of war.
Their soiled and ragged banners droop, as if
Ashamed at their defeat they could not wave,
But hung their heads and mourned their sad disgrace.
Poor fellows !   I can feel and grieve for them.
Alas ! that it is so.   That in their shame
And sorrow should our joy and triumph be.
Christian and civilized we call ourselves ;

But still barbarian in heart remain ;
Our culture mostly in the garbs we wear,
In names and forms and immaterial shows,
Merely a more elaborate barbarism.
    Anna.   I knew this music from the first—far off.
I've heard him sing it when in happy mood.
Perhaps he come with them and bids them play it.
There come the students yonder.   He'll be there.
They wave their banners to us, but pass on—
He's not among them.   I would know his step
Amidst a myriad of marching men.
Here come the wounded.   Heaven help me now,
Should he be one of them.

    Enter mournful music and then a train of wounded and dead.
        They continue passing along.

                    Be still my heart.
I must be calm and patiently await
Whatever Heaven brings of joy or woe.
But oh ! good Heaven ! if it may be thy will,
Spare him to me.   Shield and protect my love,
And save him for his country and for me.
    Dr John.   This is the price that ever must be paid
For victory and glory.   Who can look
On scene like this and ever more desire
War's guilty laurels dripping thus with blood.
A temple should be reared of human bones
And skulls dug from earth's thousand battle-fields,
As Timour reared his horrid pyramids;
And there should be entombed the conquerors,
Who for mere glory or for selfish ends
Do stir up wars, and in it they should lie
For all the ages, as they glided by,
To heap their curses and their scorn upon.
And there too I would have an image reared,
Feeding on human flesh and quaffing blood.
And I would name it Glory, martial Fame,
That there the fools that worship it may see
The hideous thing they pay their homage to.
Glory ! the idol of barbarians 'tis ;
The ignorant and brutal worship it.
It is a Moloch fed with human blood ;

Its priests the conquerors and men of war,
Who heap its horrid sacrifices up,
And pour to it its dark libations forth,
The tears and blood which they do cause to flow.
 Anna. Father! you mean not these poor wounded men,
Who thus have suffered in their country's cause?
 Dr John. No, they the victims are, the noble ones,
Who have been basely, foully sacrificed.
The monsters I condemn, the rulers are,
Who have betrayed them to this cruel fate.
All honor to the loyal citizen,
Who for his country in its need goes forth,
To battle for its freedom and its rights.
The patriot, who fights for liberty,
And at his country's call, in its defence,
Pours forth his blood, a blessed martyr is.
With noble death he crowns a noble life.
Holy should be the ground where he is laid.
Let monumental marble mark the spot,
And ever let the people there repair,
To strow with choicest flowers the soldier's grave,
And from full hearts in song and eulogy,
Unto their spirits doubtless hovering near,
Return the nation's gratitude and praise.
 Anna. Father! These wounded soldiers will need care
And gentle tendance in their helplessness;
May I not go unto the hospitals
And minister unto them in their need?
Surely the daughters of the land should nurse
The sons, who risk their lives in its defence,
And who lie bleeding helpless in their wounds.
 Dr John. Aye! beautiful and blessed is such task.
A nations highest duty it should be,
Its holiest religion, e'er to care
For those brave ones who bleed in its defence.
And old age too, whose day of battle's o'er,
May aid in the good work. All that we have
And all that we can do we will devote
Unto these bleeding heroes. Let us haste,
We'll go together to this blessed work.
      Exit Dr John into the house

Anna. There come a troop of students. He's not there.
I'd know him in the crowd, as I would mark
A stately pine towering amidst the grove.
We'll haste unto the hospital.   Perhaps
He's there wounded and helpless.   Oh dear Frank !
My love ! my life !   Where can I find you now ?
Save him, good Heaven ! and bring him back to me.
Or if that may not be, take me to him.

       Exit into the house.

Enter Mark, Ernest and Students from the procession with the body of Frank.

Mark. This is the house.   'Tis here they live.
They were his dearest friends, whom he did love.
He told us if he fell to bring him here.
The door is open.   Bear the body in.

They carry the body into the house.   A pause and then a shriek is heard within.

Mark. A heart burst in that cry.
Ernest. 'Twas she he loved.

       Curtain falls.

ACT V.—SCENE II.

In the Palace.   Enter Dr. JOHN, ERNEST and JULIAN.

Ernest. It was a mighty victory.
Dr John.   Give him
The years of Cæsar and with his renown
He'll gild a brighter page than Cæsar's is.   [this din
Julian. What speak you of ?   What mean these shouts,
Of bells and bellowing of artillery ?
Ernest. It is in honor of the victory.
Julian. What victory ?
Ernest.   Have you not heard of it ?
I thought fame had so bruited it abroad,
That every mortal ear did ring with it.
Last night, the self same hour the old king died,
After they had proclaimed the Princess Queen,
Amid'st glad acclamations, Paul arrayed

The citizens and students with the troops,
And swiftly led them 'gainst the enemy,
That were encamped without the city walls.
Ere dawn he held the heights about the foe,
And girt him round as with a wall of fire.
The roar of battle with the morning rose,
Such battle as we read of in old times,
When heroes fought for freedom and each arm
Scattered its legions.   Soon the routed foe
Begging their lives piteous laid down their arms,
And our young hero conqueror, e'en now
Returning to the city. thus is hailed
With shouts of triumph by the exultant crowd.

Exeunt Dr. John and Ernest.

Julian.   We're merely puppets in the hands of Fate,
And most fantastic tricks it plays with us.
Last night assassin, now a conqueror,
With glory won and an immortal name!
Life is a medley for mad men to play ;—
It is a strange, weird, wondrous harmony,
Given to us poor players, all untaught,
To play on instruments, so delicate,
So frail and easily jarred out of tune,
That sad, mad work we needs do make of it,—
And though we now and then may catch some strain
Of the sweet heavenly melody, yet ah!
'Tis mostly jarring and harsh dissonance.
Well! well, or sweet, or harsh I'll grind it through.
He's playing well his part, I'll play mine too.
I'll watch my chance and in his very top
Of triumph I will hurl the charge at him,
And brand him as a murderer ; or else
I'll stab and try on him the game he played
Upon the King.   Who are these coming here ?

*Re-enter Dr. John and Ernest.   Then enter Mark and Soldiers with
Captive Officers, Banners &c., &c.   They pass to one side.*

Dr. John.   These are the banners of the enemy,
Taken in fight—trophies of victory.
That is the General.   His star has paled
Before this newly risen meteor
Of ours.   These are the officers.

Ernest.   They come
To yield their swords and learn what terms of grace
The Queen will grant to them. Lo! there comes Paul.
He's lost in musing. Let us stand aside
And not disturb him in his reverie.

      Enter PAUL.

 Paul. 'Tis not for fame or greatness that I care,
To be a giant or of mind or limb,
And hold the world in wonder of my might.
But could I speak to men some true high word,
To do them good,—some pure immortal thought,
That might survive me in the minds of men,
I'd rather dying speak that single word,
Than have the mightiest sceptre given me,
That conqueror ever wielded over earth.

   Enter the PRINCE. *He gives* PAUL *a letter.*

 Prince. Here is a message to you from the Queen.
She bade me come and place it in your hand.
She will in person shortly follow it.   [thanks!
 Paul (*reading.*) She thanks me for the victory. Her
Oh sweet reward! More precious 'tis to me,
Than e'en the glory of the victory.
She bids me make such treaty with the foe,
As I deem best and most effectual
For the true weal and honor of the realm.
Well! I've a plan of treaty with the foe,
That will dispose of him effectually.
Where are the prisoners?
 Ernest.   They yonder stand,
Awaiting your commands.
 Paul.   Let them advance.

   General and Officers come forward.

 General. Thy genius and the fate of war make us
Your prisoners. Sadly we yield our swords;
Yet 'tis a solace in surrendering them,
That we may place them thus in hero hands.

    He offers his sword to Paul.

 Paul. Take back thy sword. Give me thy hand
It is thy heart I'd have thee yield to me   [instead.
And not thy weapon. It is victory,

Nobler to win, captive to love, the soul,
Than 'tis to take body prisoner.
Go lead your armies back unto their homes,
With all their arms and ancient glories decked ;
I would not pluck an honor from their brows,
But prouder than they came would send them back.
And tell them, henceforth we will strive with them,
Not in vile brutish deeds of hate and blood
And mutual injury, but in proud works,
That make the nations blest,—in strife for good,
In competition of the beautiful,
And rivalry of grand beneficence,
And all high aims, that liken earth to Heaven.
And henceforth say, that you have conquered us
And gained o'er us a glorious victory,
More glorious, than if you'd heaped our fields
With bodies of our slaughtered citizens,
When by some generous deed of blessed peace,
You shall excel what we shall do for you.
Go, sir ! You're free to march whene'er you list.
    General. It is no wonder thou didst conquer us.
    Dr John. This is a new sight 'neath the sun and one
He'll joy to see.
    The Prince.   'Tis the new era dawned,
The beam that heralds the millenium.
    Ernest. A fitting climax to his victory !
Like Ossa piled on Pelion he heaps up
Great deeds.
    General.   It is a double conquest. Thus
Do I surrender unto thee.

        He throws himself into Paul's arms.

    Dr John. How mean to this a Roman triumph were,
In its poor pompous vanity ! How few
The conquerors, who know how to improve
Truly their victories ! What sad mistakes
History records of famous battle-fields !
What opportunities of glory lost
By the vain vulgar victors ! *   *   *   *
    *   *   *   *   Ah Sedan !
Poor copy now of Jena ! what renown
Might have been thine, glory unparalleled

And all thine own, if great of soul, as strong
Of arm, had been thy conquerors !
   Julian (aside.) I now would brand him as a murderer,
But I do fear, that midst his minions here,
He'll have me seized and silenced and his word
And present influence will far outweigh
My evidence.   I'll act more daringly.
I'll stab him first with a sure fatal stroke,
And then proclaim him as a murderer.
And I'll so prove his crime, when he lies low,
'Twill justify me to the gentle Queen,
For killing him, the assassin of her sire.
Mayhap I'm like the Indian, who to drag
His rival down, did with him throw himself
Over the precipice.   Yet so be it.
Die, murderer !

               He rushes at and stabs Paul.

   Paul.   God !   Didst thou let him ?   Didst
Thou mean it so ?   'Tis so.   My work is done.
I die.   (*He falls.*)   [him ?
   Prince.   What hast thou done?   Didst mean to murder
   Ernest.   He's stabbed and murdered him !
   Mark.   Let's kill him too.
No business out of hell has such a fiend.

               He rushes at Julian but is held back.

   Julian.   I do accuse him as a murderer.
He killed the King.   He's the King's murderer.
   Ernest.   Assassin !   liar !   Would that thou didst have
A thousand lives, that we might torture them.
There shall be vengeance.   Heaven !   thou art not Heaven
If thou dost let this deed go unavenged.

               Enter the Queen, Pauline and attendants.

   Queen.   What angry noise is this?   What means this scene?
   Prince.   Alas the foulest and most mournful deed,
That ever in the course of time was done,
In all its lists of crime, has now been wrought.
   Ernest.   Most fiendishly he has been stabbed and slain.
   Pauline, (*kneeling by Paul.*)
My brother !   stabbed !   slain !   Dead is he ?
Brother !   Paul !   would that I could die with thee.

Queen. Dead! oh! no, say not dead. Is there no hope?
Paul! speak to me. My hero! 'Tis thy Queen
Doth kneel by thee and bid thee speak to her.
Still art thou? Not one word? I am thy Queen
And I'll avenge thee. Who was't did this deed?
　　Ernest. Here's the assassin. Cruel bloody fiend!
Let him be seized and with fierce tortures racked.
　　Julian. Most gracious Queen! I do confess myself
The slayer of this man. It was this hand,
That struck the blow, by which his blood pours forth.
But 'twas because he is a murderer,
The murderer of your father, most just Queen!
That I did strike the blow. Let me be tried
And I will demonstrate by certain proofs,
That he did kill the King most treacherously,
While on his bed, helpless in his old age
And innocent sleep he slumbered. When I saw
Him here exulting, haughty in his crime,
Justice compelled my arm and I did rush
And strike the blow, that laid him there.
Let me be tried and by resistless proofs
I will make certain all that I proclaim
And prove him your great father's murderer.
　　Queen. Alas! Can this be so?
　　　　　　　She swoons and falls.
Prince. 　　　　　Let her be carried hence.
　　　The attendants carry the Queen out.
　　Ernest. Infinite liar! villain! murderer!
Thou hast most foully slain him, wouldst thou now
Attack his pure and stainless character?
Why did he not, most august Prince, prefer
This dastard accusation while Paul lived,
And could with his least word repel the lie?
Why did he basely murder him, and then
Baser than murder make this fiendish charge.
　　Jul. Could he now speak I'd charge the same to him,
As I do o'er his mute and lifeless form.
Ha! he doth stir. Behold! he doth revive.
Now let the charge be plainly put to him
And see what he will answer.
　　Paul (reviving) 　　　　What means this?

Why am I here ? My scattered thoughts return.
My Prince ! beloved sister ! Ernest ! friends !
I can but say farewell unto you all.
 Pauline. Paul ! speak to me a word. Make but a sign.
This wicked fiend, who stabbed thee, makes the charge
That thou didst kill the King. Give us a sign,
If thou canst speak not, that the charge is false.
 Ernest. Aye baseless as 'tis base and dastardly.
 Paul. Does he accuse me ? Does he make such charge?
 Julian. Aye, sir ! that thou art the King's murderer.
 Prince. Beloved friend ! speak but a word. 'Tis not
That we need proof to disbelieve the lie,
Or doubt of thy most perfect innocence ;
But we would have thy word, that it may whelm
The fiend in utter and resistless scorn.
 Paul. Ernest ! my Prince ! I'm not a murderer.
 Ernest. There villain ! liar ! said I not 'twas so ?
We'll draw the falsehood blistering from thy lips.
I'd stake my soul and all its hopes of Heaven,
Upon his pure and perfect innocence,
No spot or stain is there on his clear soul. [ter ! I
 Paul. Hush ! Ernest ! Raise me friends ! Dear sis-
Will speak to you as I must soon to Him, the Judge,
To whom I'm hasting. I did say
That I was not a murderer,—and yet
It is most true, dear friends ! the King did die
Beneath my hand. The murderer is he,
Who strikes in malice ; but my act was born
Of a most holy motive and was wrought
In pure love to my country and the world.
He's gone, where soon I'll meet him and I'd speak
Not harshly of the dead, but you do know,
He was a tyrant and did crush the land,
He should have ruled in love, most grievously
Under his heavy tyranny ; and all
His God given powers he did pervert and use
For basest and most wicked purposes.
The subject and the citizen, if they
Do violate the law, unto that law
Must give account and bear its penalty.
But when our kings and rulers, they who are
The sworn and trusted guardians of the State,

The ministers of justice and of law,
When they do trample on that law and use
Their powers to base and selfish ends, there's none
To call them to account, but God alone
Or the true patriot. who fearlessly
And for his country in stern righteousness
Will greatly dare and strike for her and Heaven.
Power is not a right,—a property;
'Tis but a trust, for sacred uses given.
If he to whom it is confided, doth
Betray his trust and use it for base ends,
It is foul treachery. A traitor he
Unto his country, to the world, to Heaven.
His crime involves and doth include all crime.
He tramples on the common rights of men.
An outlaw he doth make himself, the mark
For every vengeful bolt Justice can hurl.
He is his country's deadliest enemy,
At war with every citizen and all
Who love her justly may stand forth in her
Defence and in his own and execute
Justice and judgment on his guilty head.
'Twas on these principles that I did act.
The deed and its results are now with Heaven.
My word is uttered. My life-work is done.
May good result from it. I die content.
    Julian.   Did I not say he would confess his crime!
Bear witness all that by his dying words
He doth convict himself and that he is
By his confession, the King's murderer.
    Prince.   His act, whate'er it be, doth not excuse
Or mitigate thy crime. Thy deed at least
Was murder, foul and wilful murder. Take
Him forth to prison.
    Dr John.   He's breathing now his last.
    Ernest.   Oh piteous lamentable sight!
    Mark.   The deed he did, though fearful it may seem
To vulgar apprehension, yet was grand
And noble, done of a most pure intent,
And such as in all cases like to it
The patriot may take for precedent.
    Ernest.   Nay that's a dangerous doctrine. Tyrants too

Can sharpen daggers keen as patriots can.
The liberators vulnerable are
As the usurpers.   Not the only one
Is Cæsar that has fallen.   Ah! how oft
For Freedom's martyred ones have wailed the nations.
Et, tu Brute! words not of mere reproach
But prophecy.   Aye, thou too, Brutus!   Thou
At last didst for thyself entreat the fate
With which thou struck'st down Cæsar and thyself
Didst on thyself avenge thy slaughtered friend.
And he whom we now mourn has drank
But of the cup he mingled.   Is it not
An usurpation, even the same wrong
That we condemn, for one unauthorized
To seize these fearful powers of life and death,
And self elected constitute himself
Both judge and executioner ?
      Dr. John.   It is a question, a most solemn one.
Yet 'tis no less a truth, a sacred truth,
That by all principles, of law and right,
The tyrants and usurpers are condemned,
As chief and basest of all criminals,
Least fit to live and most deserving death.
Let the world's rulers, Kings and Emperors
And Presidents be made to understand,
That 'tis not for themselves, their powers
Are given them, not for their pleasure, pomp,
Or glory, but the people's good,—the peace,
The culture and well being of the millions.
And in this sacred trust, if they prove false,
Guilty they stand before the world condemned,
Of traitors chief, of malefactors worst,
And the most criminal of criminals.
      Prince.   So do I deem : and I do hold myself
Accountable to these same principles,
That by his dying words and living act
Our friend has taught to us.   If in the place
I hold in the State, I do abuse my powers,
Or bend them to base uses, then may each
Of you be true unto your country, as
He was, and in my bosom seek a sheath
For all your weapons.   What noise was that ?

Enter an Officer.

Officer. The citizens in wild excitement rush
About the Palace and tumultuously
They do lament the fate of him they loved.
And when they saw Count Julian, as he came
Forth midst the guards, they tore him from the troops
And in their rage did rend him into pieces.   [seem,
  Dr John. The lightnings of God's justice, though they
Oft to fly wildly, yet strike hard and sure.
There is no tool that's used but does His work.
  Ernest. He's passing now away.   (*Paul dies.*)
  Prince.   Alas ! He's gone.   [you.
  Pauline. Paul ! Brother ! would that I might die with
  Prince. The pearly gates are swinging for him now.
  Mark. There'll ne'er a purer spirit enter them.
  Dr John. 'Tis well to sorrow for the noble dead ;
And tears are manly now.   For when
A great, pure spirit passes hence from earth,
It is as if a light, sought of all eyes
On high, should go out to be seen no more.
And this our natural grief would endless be
And without solace, but that we have faith
In God, that though man dies, He ever lives ;
And that in Him, souls evermore will be
Replenished of His spirit with the power
Of greatness and of goodness.   Hence we know
Even as stars arise fast as stars set,
Great men will come in place of those that die,
And earth be never left without its lights,
Its guides and teachers.   They who greatly live
Do never wholly die or pass away ;
For though their forms may vanish from our sight,
Their lips no more breath music in our ears,
Yet in their deeds they live, their works survive,
Their words ring echoing through the centuries.
Still fights the Spartan at Thermopylae,
Still Milton lives immortal in his song,
And where'er Freedom lifts its banner high,
There Washington, its foremost champion
Still aids to win conquests for liberty.
                                        Exeunt.

www.ingramcontent.com/pod-product-compliance
Lightning Source LLC
Chambersburg PA
CBHW031445270326

41930CB00007B/878